The Practitioner Inquiry Series

Marilyn Cochran-Smith and Susan L. Lytle, *SERIES EDITORS*

Inside City Schools: Investigating Literacy in the Multicultural Classroom
SARAH WARSHAUER FREEDMAN, ELIZABETH RADIN SIMONS, JULIE
SHALHOPE KALNIN, ALEX CASARENO, and the M-CLASS TEAMS

Class Actions: Teaching for Social Justice in Elementary and Middle School
JoBETH ALLEN, Editor

Teacher/Mentor: A Dialogue for Collaborative Learning
PEG GRAHAM, SALLY HUDSON-ROSS, CHANDRA ADKINS, PATTI McWHORTER,
& JENNIFER McDUFFIE STEWART, Editors

Teaching Other People's Children: Literacy and Learning in a Bilingual Classroom
CYNTHIA BALLENGER

Teaching, Multimedia, and Mathematics: Investigations of Real Practice
MAGDALENE LAMPERT & DEBORAH LOEWENBERG BALL

Tensions of Teaching: Beyond Tips to Critical Reflection
JUDITH M. NEWMAN

John Dewey and the Challenge of Classroom Practice
STEPHEN M. FISHMAN & LUCILLE McCARTHY

"Sometimes I Can Be Anything": Power, Gender, and Identity in a Primary
Classroom
KAREN GALLAS

Learning in Small Moments: Life in an Urban Classroom
DANIEL R. MEIER

Interpreting Teacher Practice: Two Continuing Stories
RENATE SCHULZ

Creating Democratic Classrooms: The Struggle to Integrate Theory and Practice
LANDON E. BEYER, Editor

Class Actions

TEACHING FOR SOCIAL JUSTICE IN ELEMENTARY AND MIDDLE SCHOOL

Edited by JoBeth Allen

FOREWORD BY CAROLE EDELSKY

Teachers College, Columbia University
New York and London

Published by Teachers College Press, 1234 Amsterdam Avenue, New York, NY 10027

Chapter 6 is adapted from "Would Queenie Be in Our Class?: Critiquing Social Inequity in Schools," by Mollie V. Trotman, *The New Advocate*, 11(1), 55–65. Reprinted by permission of Christopher-Gordon Publishers.

The appendix, "Education for Democracy," by Carole Edelsky, is reprinted from the April 1994 issue of *Language Arts*, by permission of The National Council of Teachers of English.

Library of Congress Cataloging-in-Publication Data

Class actions : teaching for social justice in elementary and middle
     school / edited by JoBeth Allen ; foreword by Carole Edelsky.
          p.   cm. — (The practitioner inquiry series)
     Includes bibliographical references and index.
     ISBN 0-8077-3857-3 (alk. paper). — ISBN 0-8077-3856-5 (pbk. :
alk. paper)
     1. Critical pedagogy—United States.   2. Social justice—Study and
teaching (Elementary)—United States.   3. Social justice—Study and
teaching (Middle school)—United States.   4. Student participation
in curriculum planning—United States.   I. Allen, JoBeth.
     II. Series.
     LC196.5.U6C53   1999
     370.11′5′0973—DC21   98-55471

ISBN 0-8077-3856-5 (paper)
ISBN 0-8077-3857-3 (cloth)

Printed on acid-free paper

Manufactured in the United States of America

06   05   04   03   02   01   00   99   8   7   6   5   4   3   2   1

Contents

Foreword

LATELY, I'VE BEEN THINKING A LOT about dark times—the Dark Ages, the Inquisition, the period of the Third Reich, the McCarthy years. Times when certain knowledge was banned and certain knowers were banished, persecuted, incarcerated, even killed. But also—and it is very important to remember this—times when a few defied the general temper, when small groups studied in hiding, when radicals risked all to save books and documents bound for burning. True, we are not living in the worst of those times. And the Literacy Education for a Democratic Society (LEADS) study group did not have to go into hiding to study unofficial and, therefore, "dangerous" ideas. But we are, alas, in different times now than we were when the general mood at least permitted, if not favored, whatever it took (as long as it didn't cost anything) to promote teacher and student empowerment. So the example of the LEADS study group is especially important now. On the one hand, it shows teachers *learning* against the grain, coming together on their own volition, without a top-down mandate, without assigned content, studying together with a common purpose. On the other hand, the common purpose it highlights—promoting democracy—runs exactly counter to the forces intent on bringing on the darkness. *Class Actions: Teaching for Social Justice in Elementary and Middle School* offers us two stories to hang onto while we've still got some light to read them by: the first, not foregrounded though impressively demonstrated, is about teachers taking control of their own professional development; the second is about teachers working with each other and with students to question injustice and inequities and, therefore, to struggle against barriers to democracy.

In order to more fully appreciate these two stories, this volume should be read with considerable awareness of the context in which it was written. The economic context in the U.S. is one where corporations are merging at record speed to produce mega-corporate entities of record size, while existing antimonopoly and antitrust laws—ordinary people's defense against such excess—are either repealed (in deregulation efforts) or ignored. As a military dictator said of Brazil in the early 1970s, "the economy is doing fine; the people aren't" (Herman, 1997, p. 20). The 500 leading corporations' profits rose 23 percent in just one year (1996), and the Gross Domestic Product increased 33 percent in 21 years (1973–1994). But in that same 21-year period, real wages fell 19 percent (Sklar, 1997). In the face of several million homeless, millions without health insurance, and millions more underemployed or trying to piece together a living wage from two or three part-time jobs so they have no home lives and no time to spend with their children, the Republicans and Democrats joined together to pass a massive tax cut. That tax cut will *save*, on average, over $16,000 per year for the top 1 percent income group (near-millionaires, millionaires, and billionaires); it will *cost* the 20 percent with the lowest incomes in the U.S. (those who qualify for welfare) about $39 per year (Lerner, 1997).

The media in the past few years have become increasingly conglomerated and globalized (Herman & McChesney, 1997). Unlike earlier periods when each city had several newspapers owned by local families, news is now packaged by a few monopolies. These monopolies have become conglomerates with major holdings not only in newspapers but also in film, television, cable, music, and book and magazine publishing. These media conglomerates, increasingly globalized so they now do one-third of their business outside the U.S., wield enormous power in shaping culture and promoting dominant ideologies (Giroux, 1997). The 1996 U.S. Telecommunications Act that deregulated the media permitted these transnational corporations to get even bigger. Not surprisingly, there was almost no press coverage of the controversies and opposition to the bill by media-watch groups.

In such a context of increasing disparities between rich and poor, of ever more benefits and power accruing to those who already control more resources, what happens to crucial public services and to the professions associated with those services? Education, it turns out, isn't the only domain to suffer. Health care in the U.S. has become largely "corporate-care" (Amsel, 1997), run by for-profit corporations whose "customers" are not patients but employers who contract for benefits. This is a system in which health care providers may well be punished financially for providing care and rewarded for withholding it. "Drive-by deliveries" and outpatient mastectomies are now common. Downsized hospital nursing staffs, sometimes comprised of minimally trained and low-wage (and, therefore, more profitable) assistants, are caring for sicker patients (those at all able to be discharged having been sent home, drains and all). Columbia, the biggest of the for-profit hospital chains, is under multiple investigations for outright fraud (Amsel, 1997). Once-public hospitals that served poor communities have been closed. The Children's Defense Fund reports that nearly 15 percent of all children have no health insurance coverage (Sklar, 1997); and those with coverage are not guaranteed treatment, as insurance companies may well deny treatment or the services of specialists for reasons of profit. Frequent negotiations of insurance contracts often require that people change physicians; there is no longer concern for the importance of established doctor–patient relationships in health care or for the role of first-hand, over-time relationships with a patient in making medical decisions.

If physicians, with their prestige (and their own drives for profit) have not been able to hold corporate greed at bay in this rapid corporatization of health care, indeed have not, by and large, even recognized the full nature of what was happening until it happened, how have educators fared in the years the LEADS group was working? The campaign against public education (Berliner & Biddle, 1995) continues—a campaign against the only social institution that might possibly dedicate itself to actively promoting democracy. As that campaign gains ground and the public loses faith in its schools, privatization efforts gain popular support. Voucher bills, easily defeated a decade ago, are passing. Charter schools are increasingly popular as legislators skip down this road toward privatization. Meanwhile, the same legislators dance circles of delay around court orders to equalize the "savage inequalities" (Kozol, 1991) in educational facilities that abound between richer and poorer school districts.

In 1997, prospects for a critically literate citizenry were dealt another blow—a rapid, intensified move to control through legislation how to think about literacy, reading, and reading instruction. In state legislatures and in Congress, legislators with no particular expertise in teaching, literacy, language acquisition, research, assessment, or any other field pertinent to learning or teaching written language decided that instruction in systematic, intensive, sequential phonics instruction was absolutely necessary in learning to read and that phonemic awareness "caused" reading. Of course, they did not come to such decisions accidentally or on their own. Particularly well-placed right-wing activists and right-wing foundations, experimentalist researchers with behaviorist views of reading, and a few publishing companies that stood to make big profits worked together as a phonics lobby to engineer those decisions. Sometimes, "working together" simply meant one person wearing multiple hats, ensuring that each "hat" pushed the same agenda. For example, Robert Sweet, former head of the Moral Majority in New Hampshire, then aide to the Republican National Party, now current head of the National Right to Read Foundation (which receives substantial funding from the Gateway Company, publisher of Hooked on Phonics), is the major staff person for the U.S. House Committee on Education and the Work Force. As such, Sweet played a key role in selecting who would testify before the Committee in early 1997 about how to think about education and literacy in the U.S., and in drafting key features of the ensuing legislation. That legislation is currently pending in the Senate (having passed the House). It indirectly establishes a national curriculum for reading instruction, emphasizing the intensive, systematic, sequential, direct instruction of phonics.

Sweet's cause was helped along considerably by the dissemination of a document (Grossen, 1997) supposedly summarizing 30 years of research on reading. Based on their own self-serving criteria, those involved in creating the document discarded all qualitative research on reading, all sociolinguistic research on reading, all teacher research on reading. Thus, what the document actually summarizes is the experimental studies of mostly NICHD-sponsored (National Institute of Child Health and Development) research on disabled readers. The policy recommendations included in the document and bought into wholeheartedly by many legislators impose one standardized curriculum on all students, despite those same politicians' cheerleading for "local control" in order to accommodate the needs and desires of different individuals. Moreover, the "30 Years" policy recommendations are poorly tied, if at all, to the findings of the original studies but derive instead from the author's a priori agenda (Allington & Woodside-Jiron, 1997). Equally bad from a research standpoint, the policy recommendations generalize to the wrong population; that is, conclusions, faulty or not, about disabled readers are generalized to *all* readers.

No matter. This document became one of the most influential policy documents of the decade. Disseminated to local district superintendents, state departments of education, state and federal legislators, agency heads, and educational decision-makers all over the U.S., it resonated with the prevailing commonsense view of what people do when they read: decode words, then comprehend. Even when confronted with evidence that the policy recommendations were not in fact drawn from the original studies, legislators and educational administrators held fast to their belief in the "scientific truth" of those recommendations (Allington & Woodside-Jiron, 1997).

The position on literacy embedded in the "30 Years" document and its legislative fallout is such a giant step backward from what has been learned about literacy that it would be laughable if it did not have so much power behind it. The federal legislation, if passed as currently written, will appropriate money for proposals for tutoring projects, professional development for teachers, revision of state certification, development of state standards for students, local instructional programs, and so on as long as the proposals are based on "reliable, replicable" research. Reliable, replicable research will be research that fits criteria to be established by a panel to be appointed by the NICHD. It is foolish to think that the panel—and its criteria—will do anything other than privilege narrow experimentalist research, thereby removing, de facto, the designation of "research" from any other type of scholarly study.

State legislation is often more direct in its mandating of one brand of phonics. In Arizona, pending legislation would mandate the number of minutes of explicitly out-of-context phonics instruction. Another bill would require teacher preparation programs to teach phonics "properly." California's new reading law is already in place. It requires consultants hired by any local school district to sign "assurances" (in essence, a loyalty oath) that they will not encourage "inventive" (*sic*) spelling or the use of "contextual clues in lieu of fluent decoding." The passage of that law in California has had a dam-breaking effect, unleashing reactionary desires to smash anything that might smack of humane practice, encouraging principals to put even more pressure on teachers to end literature discussions and focus on direct instruction in order to raise test scores, emboldening one large conservative school board to throw out bilingual education and, in its place, mandate three hours of a structured phonics program (Open Court) for kindergartners.

The transnational corporate conglomerate media have been playing their part in this latest assault on the possibilities for more educated citizens and for increased democracy. This fall (and earlier), the print and broadcast media have had one storyline in news articles about reading: schools aren't teaching kids to read because they have switched to teaching with whole language methods; the only two methods are phonics and whole language; the only important issue in literacy education is which method works best; the most important thing teachers need to know is methods; research proves that phonics beats whole language; the proof is in the test scores; test scores offer the best way to know how well someone reads. While media reports almost always (mis)quoted a whole language spokesperson, the headlines and thrust of a spate of articles that appeared in 1996–97 offered slightly different versions of all or some part of that one storyline. No major media outlet seriously questioned whether kids were really not learning to read, whether most teachers had indeed opted for whole language, what "teaching whole language" meant, whether phonics and whole language were the only ways of thinking about reading, whether reading tests test reading, and so on. Indeed, attempts to shift that storyline failed utterly, never making it into print or airspace.

Even the controversy over the federal legislation—which might have forced a look at such questions—was not reported, an absence that is especially remarkable when tied to another "coincidence." In a two-week period, four major national magazines (*Time, Newsweek, U.S. News and World Report*, and *Atlantic Monthly*) had multipage (space, that is, was not the reason for omission) feature stories on or related to reading instruction. Is reading instruction such a hot topic that the major newsweeklies all cover it in the same short period, yet fail to mention the bills on reading instruction being acted upon by Congress at the same time? It seems difficult to explain this as anything other than an implicit or explicit media-wide decision to black out this news, to suppress a different story line. Without e-mail—the new underground press—details of this legislative activity would have reached even fewer people.

If there was one storyline for news articles about reading instruction, that line did not hold for feature stories about good schools (which entail good reading instruction). The media applauded an award-winning Arizona teacher (who happens to be a well-known whole language teacher); the real-world (versus test score) successes of Central Park East (a school that takes a very different view of reading and assessment from that embedded in the media's insistent storyline about reading); and Reggio Emilia (see Edwards, Ganini, & Forman, 1996), an approach to early childhood education that focuses on symbolic representation in many media and that avoids imposing one curriculum for literacy learning on all children. The media has booed the 1987 California Language Arts Framework as if it were the villain in a bad melodrama, responsible for California's in-the-cellar test scores. At the same time, it ignores Maine, doing to the hilt what the California Framework urged and then grabbing the gold ring in test scores (Power, personal communication, 1997). The ironies—or contradictions, or maybe just one-hand's-not-knowing, etc.—abound.

All that—and more—comprise the context for the LEADS study group's work, and the context for reading CLASS ACTIONS. In the midst of an accelerating unraveling of safety nets and increasing gaps between richest and poorest, in the midst of the strongest attacks in this century on public education, in the midst of mostly-likely-to-succeed ultraconservative efforts to control what is learned and taught—in the midst of all that is this small group of educators determined to go against this tide, to pursue their own questions, to help undo rather than support reigning systems of dominance that make democracy impossible. True, these educators (who continue to meet regularly to study critical literacy and democracy-*promoting* pedagogy) have not yet been able to find ways to get their students to investigate in a sustained fashion the systematic structural nature of domination and subordination, the intricate yet concrete, institutionalized workings of *systems* of privilege. JoBeth Allen and I have talked often about how difficult it is, in the present context, to address dominance at all, let alone address it as something more than a matter of the attitudes of individuals. I know first-hand how much easier it is, as Rob Koegel (1997) says, to write about dominance than to explore it in classrooms. The educators continuing to meet as LEADS are still grappling with teaching students to investigate the detailed workings of *systems* of dominance, *systematic* inequalities, *systemic* power imbalances. What they write about here is their goals-in-progress, their efforts-so-far. Each writer is honest, disclosing hesitations, student resistance, and failures, as well as satisfactions and successes. And each is remarkably courageous, taking (and narrating) the considerable risks required (given the current context) when committing oneself to teach for democracy.

The work of the LEADS study group is one glimmer of light in darkening times. It gives me hope.

Carole Edelsky

REFERENCES

Allington, R., & Woodside-Jiron, H. (1997). *Adequacy of a program of research and of a "research synthesis" in shaping educational policy.* Report Series 1.15, National Research Center on English Learning and Achievement, State University of New York–Albany.

Amsel, L. (1997). Corporate healthcare. *Tikkun, 12*(3), 19–26, 76–77.

Berliner, D., & Biddle, B. (1995). *The manufactured crisis.* Reading, MA: Addison-Wesley.

Edwards, C., Ganini, L., & Forman, G. (1996). *The hundred languages of children.* Norwood, NJ: Ablex.

Giroux, H. (1997). Disney, Southern Baptists, and children's culture. *Z Magazine, 10*(9), 47–51.

Grossen, B. (1997). *30 years of research: What we now know about how children learn to read.* Commissioned by The Center for the Future of Teaching and Learning, Santa Cruz, CA, http:/cft.org/30years/30years.html#bibliography.

Herman, E. (1997). The economics of the right. *Z Magazine, 10*(7/8), 19–25.

Herman, E., & McChesney, R. (1997). *The global media: The new missionaries of corporate capitalism.* Herndon, VA: Cassell Academic.

Koegel, R. (1997). Beyond tolerance: Diversity, dominance, and social justice. *Democracy & Education, 12*(1), 2–3.

Kozol, J. (1991). *Savage inequalities.* New York: Crown.

Lerner, M. (1997). Piggery in America. *Tikkun, 12*(5), 7–10.

Power, B. (1997). Personal communication.

Sklar, H. (1997). Imagine a country. *Z Magazine, 10*(7/8), 65–71.

Acknowledgments

OUR STUDENTS HAVE TRULY BEEN our teachers, and we are grateful to them. We appreciate our LEADS colleagues, past and present, as well as other teachers who have dialogued with us about that elusive but essential intersection of progressive education, democratic pedagogy, and social justice. We appreciate initial support from the National Reading Research Center's School Research Consortium, PR/Award No. 117A20007 from the Office of Educational Research and Improvement, U.S. Department of Education (although this book does not reflect the position or policies of these agencies). That funding allowed us to share our work at meetings of the American Educational Research Association and the National Reading Conference, where we received valuable feedback from educators around the country. The team at Teachers College Press has been most supportive: Series Editor Susan Lytle provided insightful suggestions for revision, and Carol Collins has guided and encouraged us every step of the way. Closer to home in the Department of Language Education at the University of Georgia, we benefited greatly from the thoughtful advice and encouragement of our colleagues Joel Taxel and Karla Möller and the careful proofreading of Anita Peck.

Class Actions

CHAPTER 1

A Community of Critique, Hope, and Action

JoBeth Allen

> Through dialogue, reflecting together on what we know and don't
> know, we can then act critically to transform reality.
>
> —Paulo Freire

WHAT ARE THE GOALS of democratic schooling? To make
sure students have a voice in decisions? To make them more informed
decision-makers? To raise social consciences? To understand social structures and address power issues? And where does literacy fit? Is there a
relationship between progressive educational practices and democratic
education? Two basic tenets of our democratic society are that an educated, literate citizenry is the best defense against tyranny and insurance
of democracy, and that public schools are the great equalizers. Two basic
tenets of progressive literacy education, specifically whole language instruction, are that literacy learning should be meaningful and that children
should have choice in what they read and write. Whole language instruction is often referred to as a highly democratic philosophy (Smith, 1989),
empowering both teachers and students by honoring their voices and
decisions. However, critical theorists have argued that while letting stu-

dents choose everything they read and write may lead to literacy being personally meaningful, unmediated choice is not likely to help students grow in their understanding of diverse cultures and opinions, or understand and address issues of social justice.

The authors of this volume formed a study group, Literacy Education for a Democratic Society (LEADS), in 1995 to explore the intersection of progressive education and democratic pedagogy. We are committed to progressive education, including whole language, and to democratic education, although we were less sure of what that might include. We are uncomfortable because our classrooms are not as democratic as we want them to be. We acknowledge the discontinuity between our beliefs and actions, and are deeply interested in what others are doing to mesh whole language instruction with democratic principles. We began with a challenge from Carole Edelsky.

EDELSKY'S CALL FOR ACTION

We do not have, and cannot have, a democracy where all people are not only created as equal but live as equals when we have systems of domination. In her 1994 article, reprinted in this book, Edelsky referred specifically to systemic privilege based on race, gender, wealth, and corporate power. "Education for bringing about democracy would aim at helping put an end to the systems of domination that create the condition we have now—a condition of decidedly unequal influence over who gets what," according to Edelsky (1994, p. 253).[1] In a true democracy, "who gets what" would be a matter of political process involving participation among equals. We often think of this distribution of rights or privileges in terms of adults: who gets financial security, fulfilling jobs, or the highest-quality health care. Those of us in schools think of equal rights in terms of children: who gets the best teachers, high-quality literature, time to read it, turns at talk, listened to, and valued socially.

Edelsky, like us, is a language educator; she is pursuing practices that would create a society *With Literacy and Justice for All* (1996). She points out that many of our progressive theories and practices, including whole language, have avoided issues of social justice. Conversely, many critical theorists haven't developed methods of pedagogy; progressive teachers and critical theorists need to talk if student choice is to have real meaning, according to Patrick Shannon (1992).

We need to retheorize language education, according to both Edelsky and Shannon, to make it serve education *for* democracy. The rights and responsibilities of students include responsibility to society. Critical theorist Henry Giroux (1992) pointed to the distinction Dewey made between education as a function of society and society as a function of education. "In other words," Giroux asked, "are schools to uncritically serve and reproduce the existing society or challenge the social order to develop and advance its democratic imperatives?" (p. 25). This challenge is in the hands of teachers.

One of our primary tools is dialogue, argue many critical educators like Paulo Freire, whose writing and teaching have profoundly influenced educators around the world (including some LEADS members). Freire (1970) contended that "without dialogue there is no communication, and without communication there can be no true education" (p. 81). Freire identified "the word" as the essence of dialogue, with the word consisting of "reflection and action" in "radical interaction." Such transformative dialogue has specific characteristics:

> Dialogue cannot exist . . . in the absence of a *profound love* for the world and for [people]. Dialogue further requires an *intense faith* in [people], faith in [their] power . . . to create and re-create, faith in [their] vocation to be more fully human . . . Nor yet can dialogue exist without *hope*. Hope is rooted in [people's] incompletion, from which they move out in constant search—a search that can be carried out only in communion with other [people]. The dehumanizing resulting from an unjust order is not a cause for despair but for hope, leading to the incessant pursuit of the humanity denied by injustice. . . . Finally, true dialogue cannot exist unless the dialoguers engage in *critical thinking* . . . thinking which does not separate itself from action, but constantly immerses itself in temporality without fear of the risks involved. (Freire, 1970, pp. 77–81, emphasis added)

In the Freirian tradition, Edelsky challenged literacy educators to engage in dialogue within two communities, our classroom communities, and "communities of colleagues" where we are committed to education for democracy. In our classroom communities, we need to create opportunities for students to examine relations among language, literacy, and power. Within communities of colleagues, Edelsky's challenge incorporates some of the elements Freire identified for dialogue. She urged educators to engage in (1) *critique*—a critical discussion of taken-for-granted issues and institutionalized decisions, (2) *hope*—learning from others who have successfully challenged undemocratic and unjust systems, and (3) *action*—doing something to further a just society. Many educators learned about whole language from teachers like Nancie Atwell and Carol Avery, who provided detailed portraits and clarifying commentary about whole language classrooms. Edelsky called for equally descriptive pictures of classrooms that have education for democracy at their center.

RESPONDING AS A COMMUNITY OF COLLEAGUES

After reading Edelsky's article, Barbara Michalove and I wrote colleagues we thought might be interested in looking at the potential intersections of progressive and democratic education. We included the article, and invited them to get together and discuss the possibility of forming a study group like Edelsky envisioned. We began in 1995 and as of this writing are still meeting; still engaging in critique, hope, and action; and still trying to understand and practice education *for* democracy.

There are teachers who make social issues central in their whole language inquiry classroom, teachers like Karen Smith, Debra Goodman, and the teachers associated with the Center for Democratic Schooling. There are specific curriculum and teaching strategies in publications such as *Radical Teacher, Teaching Tolerance,* and *Rethinking Schools.* For example, Linda Christensen's (1994) students critique cartoons on television and in movies for issues of gender, race, and class. Bill Bigelow and Bob Peterson (1994) teach critical literacy by showing their students how to detect textbook omissions and biases. There are excellent examples of whole schools based on democratic principles (e.g., Goodman, 1992; Meier, 1995). However, we wanted to explore what we could do to democratize our own classrooms.

We gathered as a community of colleagues from elementary schools, middle schools, and teacher educaton programs in the Athens, Georgia, area. Some participants have come for only one or two discussions; others have participated from the beginning, but chose not to write for this book. All of us are trying to go beyond the "how to" of literacy to explore the "what for." Table 1.1 lists chapter authors and their teaching roles at the time they wrote for this book.

We met every two weeks during the summer of 1995 for "critique, hope, and action"; since then we have met approximately once a month at different members' homes. As part of the process of getting to know each other, we shared potluck dinners and life stories, including influences and experiences involving social issues and activism. Each of the following chapters includes relevant portions of that history. We drew on the educative research process developed by Andrew Gitlin and a group of teachers in Utah (Gitlin et al., 1992), which emphasizes the relationship between personal history and the research questions researchers pursue. The Utah teachers learned, within a framework of critical theory, that research was most important for them when they identified recurring issues in their own lives. While we did not follow the educative research model explicitly, we did decide that it was important to start with ourselves, and why we wanted to be a part of this study group.

Table 1.1. Information on Chapter Authors

Name	Level	Experience	Role	Workplace Demographics	Author's Ethnicity
JoBeth Allen	Teacher educator, elementary language arts	Teacher education, 10 years	Professor	Predominantly White, public university	European American
Barbara Michalove	4th grade	K–4, 17 years	Teacher	Mixed Black/Hispanic/White, urban, low SES	European American
Tricia Taylor	4th grade	No teaching experience	Student teacher	Mixed White/Black, rural, low SES	European American
Jane West	Teacher educator, elementary language arts and social studies	2 years	Assistant professor	All-female, predominantly White, private liberal arts college	European American
Jill Wilmarth, Cathy Crumley, Julie Dickerson, Melissa Francis	Undergraduate students in teacher preparation program	No teaching experience	Seniors in education courses	All-female, predominantly White, private liberal arts college	European American
Karen Hankins	1st grade	Kindergarten, 10 years	Teacher	Multicultural, suburban and urban, mixed SES	European American
Mollie Blackburn	6th grade, "gifted" language arts	"Regular" language arts, 4 years	Teacher	Mixed White/Black, urban, mixed SES	European American
Eurydice Bauer	Teacher educator, elementary reading	Teacher education, 2 years	Assistant professor	Predominantly White, public university	Haitian American
Suzanne McCotter	6th grade, all subjects	School media specialist; teacher, 5 years	Team teacher with Sara Glickman	Mixed Black/White, rural/urban, mixed SES	European American
Sarah Johnson	6th grade special education	Special education, 16 years	Teacher	Mixed Black/White, rural, low SES	European American

Note: Other LEADS members during the first three years included Carolyne Burgman, Clarke Middle School media specialist; Fenice Boyd, Language Education, University of Georgia; Emily Carr, 2nd grade teacher at Fourth Street Elementary; Susan Taylor, 1st grade teacher from Sylvania Elementary School; Sara Glickman, 6th grade team teacher with Suzanne at Coile Middle School; Tina Pippin, Religious Studies at Agnes Scott College; and Julie Wiesberg, Science/Math Education, Agnes Scott College.

Our "activist autobiographies" took various forms, from brief notes to extended narratives. We reflected on various influences in our lives, including parents, schooling, home communities, and college years. We learned that several of us had a family member who encouraged involvement in social issues, by words and/or example. We defined activism or interest in issues of social justice very broadly; for example, environmental activism included starting an urban organic gardening coop, recycling, and living in a solar-powered house in the 1970s. We laughed at ourselves as we debated whether boycotting tuna, writing letters to the editor, and rescuing stray dogs counted; we squirmed a bit when we compared our current involvement with our 1960s ideals. Some members identified themselves as "work-quietly-in-the-background" people, others as more "front-line" activists.

The need to do more in our classrooms, to be more intentional about advancing democracy, drew us together. While we had a range of past experiences and current teaching situations, there were common threads:

- We wanted to be a part of a group that talked about education. LEADS was a place to get feedback on decisions ("So how democratic is my classroom?"), to discuss ideas, to reflect on our own teaching, to learn from each other's practice, or simply to connect with other educators.
- We wanted to create more equitable classrooms, and it was enlightening to see that some of the issues are exactly the same for 8-year-old students as for 28-year-old students ("What do I do when they *don't* take responsibility for their learning?").
- We wanted to teach our students to question the world the way it is, to discuss their roles in addressing social issues, and to give them the tools to make the world a better place.

We read extensively that first summer. We selected books, articles, and chapters from a pooled collection of readings related to education for democracy. Each member selected readings that were important to her and discussed them at the next meeting; when one of us recommended something to the whole group, we all read it. We subscribed to, read, and had some of our best discussions around articles in the periodicals *Teaching Tolerance*, available free to educators from the Southern Poverty Law Center, and *Rethinking Schools*. A compilation from the latter, *Rethinking Our Classrooms: Teaching for Equity and Justice* (Bigelow, Christensen, Karp, Miner, & Peterson, 1994), was so relevant that we ordered personal copies.

One of the most helpful, as well as enjoyable, meetings was in the middle school library where member Carolyne Burgman is the media specialist. Each of us brought our personal collection of children's and adolescent literature related to social issues. We "book talked," borrowed, and made a categorized resource list for ourselves with over 200 titles. This became an ongoing feature of our meetings, as members found additional children's and young adult books throughout the year.

Toward the end of summer, after reading what other teachers had accomplished, we began to plan specific teaching actions for our public school and university classes. We spent hours discussing both processes and content: What did democratic classrooms look like? What was important to students, to us, to society—and how did we balance these? How could we support student voices in decision-making and still provide the leadership we knew to be essential? How could we integrate social justice issues into the curriculum? What books did we want students to read, what issues did we want them to study, and how could we develop democratic processes for studying social issues?

Our discussions were not about the important and intriguing distinctions theorists make among various democracies, for example, liberal, radical, and critical. We started with Edelsky's focus on what teachers can do in classrooms with critical analysis of social issues through literature discussion and other focused studies. Because we did not start with a definition of democracy, multiple interpretations evolved. At one of our early meetings, we actually looked up the term in Webster's dictionary. As a group, we were interested both in the process of democracy ("government by the people; the people considered as a source of political authority") and the unfulfilled promise of social justice in a democracy ("a social condition of equality and respect for the individual within the community"). The group frequently discussed the sometimes conflicting relationship between establishing democratic processes and addressing social issues.

Our ongoing exploration of the complexities, differing interpretations, and challenges of democracy are both age-old and vitally current. John Dewey (1938/1963), in his emphasis on experiential education that underlies many progressive educational practices today, wrote:

> There is, I think, no point in the philosophy of progressive education which is sounder than its emphasis upon the importance of the participation of the learner in the formation of the purposes which direct his [or her] activities in the learning process, just as there is no defect in traditional education greater than its failure to secure the active co-operation of the pupil in construction of the purposes involved in his [or her] studying. But the meaning of purposes and ends is not self-evident and self-explanatory. (p. 67)

In other words, it is critical that students have their own purposes for learning, but how do they generate those purposes, and what makes them meaningful? As you will read in Suzanne McCotter's chapter, "having a say" through 6th graders' class meetings was integral to her democratic classroom, but an open forum in and of itself did not lead to involvement in curriculum and student learning processes. Likewise, Jane West's college students didn't just have more decision-making in their teacher preparation course, they had the responsibility to design curriculum that was meaningful. What were Suzanne's and Jane's roles? What are our roles? Ira Shor posed a similar question to Paul Freire in their dialogues on transforming education (Shor & Freire, 1987):

> In the U.S., one school of progressive thought seeks to develop "self-directed learners." In this pedagogy, the teacher is a "resource-person" ... Students are expected to design their own learning contracts and to be responsible enough to follow them and to ask for help. . . . [E]ducators will point to the self-directed learner as an empowered student.
>
> Paulo: But it is not my conception of democracy and empowerment! . . . For me education is always directive, always. The question is to know towards what and with whom is it directive . . . I don't believe in self liberation. Liberation is a social act. . . . [I]f you are not able to use your recent freedom to help others to be free by transforming the totality of society, then you are exercising only an individualist attitude towards empowerment or freedom. (p. 109)

Freire responded by elaborating on the role of the liberating teacher as one who directs serious study of social and political issues, explaining that this position is "a radical democratic one because it attempts directiveness and freedom at the same time, without authoritarianism by the teacher and without license by the students" (p. 171).

We agreed that we have to be more than "resources" if we are to teach for democracy; we have been trying to figure out just what role to take in various circumstances. What gives the teacher the right, indeed the responsibility, to guide students in making important decisions, in creating meaningful curricula that address the American society as a whole, as well as their roles in society? According to our colleague Carl Glickman, a Jeffersonian scholar who has written extensively about "education *as* democracy,"

> Public education is the only institution designated and funded as the agent of the larger society in protecting the core value of its citizenry: democracy. The essential value of the public school in a democracy, from the beginning, was to ensure an educated citizenry capable of participating in discussions,

debates, and decisions to further the wellness of the larger community and protect the individual right to "life, liberty, and the pursuit of happiness." (Glickman, 1993, pp. 8–9)

DIALOGUE ABOUT DEMOCRACY: ISSUES, ACTIONS, AND GROUP CONCERNS

As the school year began, we spent less time reading (out of necessity) and more time on what and how we were teaching, how students were responding, and what advice group members could offer for specific situations. It was most helpful to have the perspectives of teachers in other schools, other grades, and regular and special education—our "immediate" teachers—as well as the perspectives of those we were reading— our "distant teachers" (John-Steiner, 1985).

Issues and Actions

Issues of how the classroom community functions dominated many meetings. We debated pullout services, inclusion, and balancing the rights and responsibilities of highly disruptive students with those of the rest of the class. Mollie's teaching assignment in the "gifted" track led to examinations of both the ills and the realities of so-called ability tracking in the Athens area, with its resulting racial tracking. The problems of European American women teaching African American children led us to read Lisa Delpit's (1994) *Other People's Children*. At Barbara's recommendation, we also read Gloria Ladson-Billings's (1994) *Dreamkeepers* and have had ongoing deliberations on how to provide more culturally relevant teaching. We discussed the costs to the African American community when schools were integrated, including the loss of thousands of African American teachers and administrators, and what we can do given that damaging legacy.

Another recurring topic was the devastating effects of poverty on many of the children we teach. A *Kappan* special report by Stephanie Coontz (1995) challenged us to reject the myth that it is the breakdown of the American family that is causing all our social ills, and to understand that "most poverty comes from our changing earnings structure, not from our changing family structure" (p. 9). When the top 1% of the population has as much income as the bottom 40%, and the gap widens each year, our society is in trouble. We saw daily the many ways this economic inequity affected children in the bottom 40%.

We reflected not only on the issues we thought important, but on those our students brought to school. In several classrooms, students were most concerned about violence or the threat of violence, as well as parental discord and/or separation. We shared class discussions, and how inadequate we felt to deal with some of the fear and anger students expressed. Many of the chapters in this volume are a result of student interests or questions (Taylor, McCotter, West, et al.) or student comments or actions that prompted their teachers to engage them in reflection and action (Michalove, Blackburn, Bauer).

Several of our talks pointed to inadequate or incomplete teacher education. It was particularly helpful to those of us with that responsibility to hear from other group members what we should be doing in both preservice and in-service courses. Eury Bauer (Chapter 7, this volume) expressed frustration with the resistance of some of her students to the emphasis she placed on issues of race, gender, culture, and power; group members urged her to convince her students that far from being extraneous, these issues are central to teaching in today's schools. In fact, the Georgia Board of Education mandated a Core Values Curriculum that included many of the issues Eury emphasized (e.g., equality, justice, liberty, and tolerance).

As a teacher educator at the same university, I shared Eury's commitment to helping prospective teachers think about their role in democratizing literacy eduction. On the advice of the group, I asked my undergraduate language arts students to generate their own value statements; they then compared them to the BOE Core Values. They found much with which they agreed (e.g., honesty, cooperation, tolerance, respect for self and others) and some interesting points for discussion ("respect for and acceptance of authority"). After responding to the Caldecott-winning *Smokey Night* (Bunting, 1994), students generated a list of social issues (e.g., violence, racism, various kinds of abuse, economic and environmental issues) related to the core values that they and the BOE had identified. Students explored the purposes of education and the relationship between literacy and democracy, and how to integrate social issues in the curriculum through children's literature and discussion strategies.

At LEADS meetings we always shared children's literature and talked about how particular books served as springboards for meaningful discussion. Emily Carr shared many examples of how she integrated social issues in prescribed curriculum units. For example, when her second graders study families, they include homeless families by reading *Fly Away Home* by Eve Bunting (1991); when they study nutrition, they read *Uncle Willie and the Soup Kitchen* (DiSalvo-Ryan, 1991); and during the study of simple machines, which takes place as students create their own inventions for Invent American, students discuss *The Gadget War* (Duffey, 1991) and *The Real McCoy* (Towle, 1993), about African American inventor Elijah McCoy. For a small group reading sports books, Emily recommended *Baseball Saved Us* (Mochizuki, 1993), introducing them to the internment of Japanese Americans during World War II.

Group Concerns

There have been two recurring tensions for us as a group: the lack of racial and gender diversity in the group, and the self-criticism that we are more talk than action.

While we knew how important it was for us to have a diversity of perspectives and experiences, the teachers we knew, and consequently invited, were mostly elementary and middle school, mostly women, and mostly European American. The group was diverse in terms of age, experience, backgrounds, and religion, but we were all women, and mostly European American. By the end of the first summer, only two members were African American; one, Fenice Boyd, was a long-distance member who suggested readings and received the minutes of the meetings, but did not move to Athens until September.

Carolyne Burgman, the other African American teacher in the group, spoke out at the last meeting of the summer. She was really troubled by the lack of diversity, citing both race and gender. She explained how often she was "the only one" on school committees, district committees, even as a parent at many of her daughters' school events. "I thought in a group like this, I wouldn't have to be the only one," she said sadly.

We all agreed. Sara Glickman suggested that we read two chapters from *Other People's Children* (Delpit, 1995) to understand why many teachers who do not belong to the dominant European American educational establishment might be reluctant to join our predominantly white group. We read and discussed Delpit's chapters "The Silenced Dialogue" and "Teachers' Voices" at the next meeting. Everyone expressed the same frustration and sense of failure. We tried to recruit men and teachers of color; however, it would be a year before Eury Bauer joined the group.

At the beginning of the group's third year, we recruited Beverly Washington, who teaches an exploratory class on cultural diversity to middle school students. After Beverly read the notes from our previous meeting, she noted that we had discussed several issues that really interested her, especially racial issues in her school and in the district. Then she asked a question that we often asked ourselves: "Do you all ever take any action, or do you just talk about things?"

As much as we valued the monthly opportunity to "just talk," as much as we believed the dialogue itself to be important in examining democratic principles and naming injustices, we knew that talk without action was very limited. In examining the talk–action pattern within LEADS, we are seeing a cycle of group dialogue and individual action. Most of the chapters in this book report action phases of the cycle. Two, Eury Bauer's and Sarah Johnson's (Chapters 7 and 9), show the dialogue-action-reflection cycle over time. A related self-criticism is that all of the enactments of democratic education we have undertaken to date have been at the individual classroom level. We are not addressing what Edelsky calls systems of domination, for example, racist policies underlying many of the injustices in our own schools. Beverly's question—"Do you ever take any action?"—has profound implications for the future of LEADS. Will we continue to take individual action, as reported in this book? Will we find a way to take collective action? What is our role in educating for democracy?

INQUIRIES INTO AND ENACTMENTS OF
EDUCATION FOR DEMOCRACY

Given the range of settings, particular students, and personal commitments, members focused on different aspects of teaching for democracy. We believed that students should be involved in making decisions in the classroom, that they would learn more if they had ownership in the learning process (see Glickman, 1993, for a review of research that supports this belief), and that classrooms are a critical arena for learning how to be citizens in a democratic society. But we also agreed with Goodlad (1997) that "disproportionate attention has been given . . . to issues of democratic governance" at the expense of serious attention to the responsibilities of individuals to society. Goodlad warned that "deviations from patriotic symbolism have stimulated more rhetorical outrage than has the plight of the poor and suffering. For a society to rest its case for the virtues of democracy on mechanisms of governance alone, however nobly framed, is to place both that society and democracy itself at risk" (1997, p. 156).

The chapters in this volume represent a collective effort to engage in and critique the complexities of democratic education. Several members developed shared decision-making processes such as team meetings and student-generated curriculum for examining social issues; we studied the responsibilities of individuals to society, and society to individuals, through investigations of privilege and prejudice. As our first year together shaped our thinking and our actions, individual inquiries into or enactments of democracy tended to fall into three overlapping areas. We have organized the book into these areas—social issues in the curriculum, schools as contributors to a more just society, and students' rights and responsibilities in making decisions about their own learning. It is our hope that readers will recognize themselves, their students, and the endless possibilities for "critique, hope, and action" in their own classrooms.

Social Issues in the Curriculum

Barbara Michalove's 4th grade class (Chapter 2) was not working well as a community: two students with severe emotional problems had frequent, disruptive outbursts; some in the majority-black population seemed intolerant of Hispanic students new to the school; several students were insensitive to the three hearing-impaired students. While Barbara had planned community involvement projects with her students, the realities of her diverse and volatile classroom dictated a very different focus. She and the students first had to create a caring, supportive community among themselves. Barbara carefully sequenced experiences that led students from examining the history of prejudice in the United States to facing their own prejudices.

Unlike Barbara's urban setting, the rural 4th grade in which Tricia Taylor student-taught (Chapter 3) was predominantly European American. Tricia held daily class meetings in which she often read books to prompt discussions of social issues; at other times, students raised issues for discussion. When one student read that her favorite author was homosexual, the class entered new terrain. Tricia had to ask herself, "At what cost will I pursue democracy and social justice? Can I hold to my principles in the face of disapproving peers and alienated students? If we believe in justice and equality, can we choose our battles?"

Eury Bauer found herself asking the same questions in teaching reading methods courses for undergraduates (Chapter 7). Many of her students, mostly middle-class European American women, have never had a teacher of color before. She emphasizes social and cultural issues as they relate to literacy teaching and learning. Eury encountered a great deal of resistance, evident both in classroom encounters and critical evaluations of her teaching—evaluations that are examined closely during both annual salary reviews and promotion and tenure decisions. However, rather than abandon these critical educational issues, she has used student resistance to develop new approaches that are making her undergraduates more responsive to her and her instructional beliefs and strategies.

In another design of teacher education for democracy, Jane West and four undergraduate students argue that teacher preparation programs need to model democratic processes that can translate to K–12 classrooms

(Chapter 4). In an integrated social studies/language arts teacher preparation program, Jane not only involved students in making decisions about their own education, she actively engaged them in an inquiry into a critical social issue: religion in the public schools. These undergraduates, in the heart of the Bible Belt, attending a religiously funded college, delved deep into an issue that was dividing Congress and the nation. They interviewed teachers, superintendents, lawyers, politicians, and activists on both ends of the political spectrum. Still, Jane struggles with a question common among activist teachers: When does a professor's focus on the study of democratic issues stop being democratic?

Schools as Contributors to a More Just Society

In a debate that is almost as fundamental as the right to a free public education in the United States, educators and citizens have argued about the role of schooling. Is it to impart the culture and values of the society, or to change that society? The authors of this volume believe that schools have the potential to help young people envision a more just society, and eventually to contribute to a more democratic community. Authors in this section examine their own prejudice and privilege, and lead their students in interrogating their privilege, and their assumptions about others.

Karen Hankins (1998) developed a teacher research methodology involving reflective memoir. In the tradition of Vivian Paley, she records and reflects on classroom discussions through the reflective lens of her childhood memories. In her chapter, Karen juxtaposes three scenes: the miseducation of children on the margins of her 1950s 2nd grade, the frustrated comments of her 1990s colleagues about "those children," and her missed opportunities to connect with her students because she hadn't understood their response to a story. Her commitment to democratic principles leads her to listen in a different way to children's conversations. How does she—how do we all—privilege certain speakers? Whose discourse patterns do we honor, and how? Karen practices a pedagogy of location, where "at question is the issue of who speaks, under what conditions, for whom, and how knowledge is constructed and translated within and between different communities located within asymmetrical relations of power" (Giroux, 1992, p. 2). This honest analysis of children's talk and one teacher's response provides the thoughtful reader with potential pathways to making classroom talk more equitable.

In Chapter 6, we learn what one teacher did when she was assigned to teach the "gifted" section of language arts at her middle school, in spite of her belief that tracking, including separate classes for advanced students, was inherently inequitable. Mollie Blackburn asked herself, and eventually her students, "Why is our class so affluent? So homogeneous? So white? Why doesn't this feel right?" She engaged her 6th graders in a study of their own privilege through a Georgia novel, *Queenie Peavy* (Burch, 1966), about a very bright girl their age who did not dress, act, or perform in school the way the "good" students did. She asked her students, "If Queenie went to this school, would she be in our class?"

For teachers to undertake the close personal reflection that led Karen and Mollie to view their classrooms as places that could contribute to a more just society, teacher preparation needs to emphasize education for democracy. In the final chapter in this section, Eury Bauer recounts the resistance she felt from some of her undergraduates when she focused on helping them meet the needs of the culturally and linguistically diverse students they would teach. Faced with both covert and overt resistance, she felt her choices were to resign, to focus only on technical content, to go on an "angry crusade," or to try to understand the students' perspective in order to share hers as a Haitian American educator and mother. It is a remarkable story of courage, commitment, and change.

Students' Rights and Responsibilities in Making Decisions About Their Own Learning

A common goal across the study group was the democratization of our own classrooms. In the chapters that focus on social issues, teachers are working to involve their students in more democratic ways: planning curriculum, choosing books, designing projects, evaluating their own work, and generally having a voice in their own education. In Chapter 8, Suzanne McCotter focuses on the daily processes of involving students in decision-making: Team Meetings. For sixth-grade students who were not used to making decisions in school, this process did not come easily. Suzanne describes how she and her co-teacher set up the Team Meetings, prepared the students to work collaboratively, and extended the responsibility for making decisions about their everyday school life (like the ubiquitous Pencil Break) to thinking critically about broader social issues in literature groups.

In Chapter 9, special education teacher Sarah Johnson is transformed by the writings of several democratic educators and consequently seeks to transform the lives of her students. She believes education for democracy is especially critical for her students, often perceived as being on the bottom rung of the social ladder (poor, mentally handicapped, from families who rarely have social status in the community), to take control of their own learning. Pathways include students learning to question, rather than just be questioned by, teachers; developing literacy skills through addressing important social issues; and participating in writing their own Individual Educational Plans.

In Chapter 10, we raise questions that continue to mark our conversations, and our lives. What impact might our individual classroom actions have beyond the classroom? What do we do when we encounter resistance from teachers, and those studying to become teachers? How do we challenge biases, in ourselves as well as in others? What actions can we take that challenge systems of domination? How can the group itself evolve to include more diverse voices and perspectives?

We have written about our experiences, our questions, our teaching and reflections on teaching, in the hope that these chapters will be a springboard for other educators. We hope to dialogue with readers in *critique* of taken-for-granted issues and institutionalized decisions; to provide *hope* through our small, local attempts to challenge undemocratic and unjust systems; and to engender *action* on the part of you, our readers, as we continue to explore ways we can act as individuals and as a group.

NOTES

The opening quote is from Shor and Freire (1987, p. 99).
1. Page numbers for Edelsky (1994) refer to the original publication.

REFERENCES

Bigelow, B., Christensen, L., Karp, S., Miner, B., & Peterson, B. (1994). *Rethinking our classrooms: Teaching for equity and justice*. Milwaukee, WI: Rethinking Schools Limited.

Bigelow, B., & Peterson, B. (1994). Students as textbook detectives. In B. Bigelow, L. Christensen, S. Karp, B. Miner, & B. Peterson (Eds.), *Rethinking our classrooms: Teaching for equity and justice* (pp. 158–159). Milwaukee, WI: Rethinking Schools Limited.

Bunting, E. (1991). *Fly away home*. New York: Clarion Books.

Bunting, E. (1994). *Smoky night*. San Diego: Harcourt Brace.

Burch, R. (1966). *Queenie Peavy*. New York: Viking Press.

Christensen, L. (1994). Unlearning the myths that bind us. In B. Bigelow, L. Christensen, S. Karp, B. Miner, & B. Peterson (Eds.). *Rethinking our classrooms: Teaching for equity and justice* (pp. 8–13). Milwaukee, WI: Rethinking Schools Limited.

Coontz, S. (1995). The American family and the nostalgia trap. Special Report, *Phi Delta Kappan, 76*(7).

Delpit, L. (1995). *Other people's children: Cultural conflict in the classroom.* New York: New Press.

Dewey, J. (1938/1963). *Experience and education.* New York: Macmillan.

DiSalvo-Ryan, D. (1991). *Uncle Willie and the soup kitchen.* New York: Morrow.

Duffey, B. (1991). *The gadget war.* New York: Viking.

Edelsky, C. (1996). *With literacy and justice for all: Rethinking the social in language and education.* London: Falmer Press.

Edelsky, C. (1994). Education for democracy. *Language Arts, 71,* 252–257. [Reprinted in this volume]

Freire, P. (1970). *Pedagogy of the oppressed.* New York: Continuum Publishing.

Giroux, H. (1992). *Border crossing: Cultural workers and the politics of education.* New York: Routledge, Chapman, and Hall.

Gitlin, A., Bringhurst, K., Burns, M., Cooley, V., Myers, B., Price, K., Russell, R., & Tiess, P. (1992). *Teachers' voices for school change: An introduction to educative research.* New York: Teachers College Press.

Glickman, C. (1993). *Renewing America's schools.* San Francisco: Jossey-Bass.

Goodlad, J. (1997). Reprise and a look ahead. In J. Goodlad & T. McMannon (Eds.), *The public purpose of education and schooling* (pp. 155–167). San Francisco: Jossey-Bass.

Goodman, J. (1992). *Elementary schooling for a critical democracy.* Albany, NY: State University of New York Press.

Hankins, K. (1998). Cacophony to symphony: Memoirs in teacher research. *Harvard Educational Review, 68,* 80–95.

John-Steiner, V. (1985). *Notebooks of the mind: Explorations of thinking.* New York: Harper & Row.

Ladson-Billings, G. (1994). *The dreamkeepers: Successful teachers of African American children.* San Francisco: Jossey-Bass.

Meier, D. (1995). *The power of their ideas: Lessons for America from a small school in Harlem.* Boston: Beacon Press.

Mochizuki, K. (1993). *Baseball saved us.* New York: Scholastic.

Shannon, P. (1992). *Becoming political: Readings and writings in the politics of literacy education.* Portsmouth, NH: Heinemann.

Shor, I., & Freire, P. (1987). *A pedagogy for liberation.* Westport, CT: Bergin & Garvey.

Smith, W. (1989). What's so democratic about whole language? *Democracy and Education, 3*(3), 1–4.

Towle, W. (1993). *The real McCoy.* New York: Scholastic.

PART I

Social Issues in the Curriculum

CHAPTER 2

Circling In: Examining Prejudice in History and in Ourselves

Barbara Michalove

I HAD A SHELTERED CHILDHOOD in a close-knit Jewish community in Atlanta, Georgia. I was sheltered, but not ignorant. It wasn't too long after the end of World War II, and I was painfully aware of the atrocities that had taken place in Europe. I remember vividly my first encounter with anti-Semitism: a large sign in a Highlands, North Carolina, neighborhood that read NO JEWS ALLOWED.

What frightened me as a child, and still does as an adult, is that the people who put up the sign in North Carolina appeared to be no different from me. If my family, religious community, or social group had been different, I could have been raised to think in the same narrow, bigoted way. Believing strongly that the relationships children have with adults influence their thinking tremendously, I began teaching with an idealism about the difference I could make in the thoughts and actions of children. Now, 20 years later, tempered by many experiences, I maintain a realistic idealism about what schools can do to create understanding and respect among the increasingly diverse citizens of our country.

My activism has been primarily through my teaching. I have chosen to teach at two schools in Athens that serve predominantly low-income families because I want to make a difference in the lives of these children.

I want to help them develop the inner strength to change their own lives. As the LEADS group read about what other teachers committed to democratic education had done in the periodicals *Rethinking Schools* (various years) and *Teaching Tolerance* (various years), I envisioned getting my students involved with the local homeless shelter, or perhaps taking on an environmental issue such as replacing the styrofoam our lunchroom used with cardboard products.

My goal was for my 4th graders to see that they could act on some aspect of social concern. I wanted them involved in something real, something outside of themselves; I had in mind beginning the school year with the book *The Kid's Guide to Social Action* (Lewis, 1991). They needed to develop a sense of their own power instead of the powerlessness they often lived with in their family situations (and as children in general). Rather than the attitude of, "I'm just a kid—I can't do anything," I wanted them to be able to say, "I really made a difference." I felt that by taking on a community issue outside our classroom they might gain that sense of power. And if they saw their power to change things in the outside world, maybe some of them would feel the possibilities of changing their own lives, instead of the fatalism and lack of self-respect, self-control, and self-determination that I observed in some students.

But even as I read and planned, I knew that I would have to get to know my students before I could go any further. That turned out to be critical, because my class came to me with a pressing need to deal with their own diversity as a learning community.

A NEED TO BUILD COMMUNITY

Fourth Street Elementary is a Title 1 school, with approximately 80% of the students qualifying for free or reduced-price meals. It is the first school in our district in 25 years that has been built in an African American neighborhood. The diverse staff began the school in 1990 with a vision: Fourth Street would be a center for the community, provide social services, and cooperate with local churches. We would build on students' strengths and emphasize African American contributions to U.S. society.

Our school houses many special education classrooms, including those for students with hearing impairments; students are mainstreamed into regular classrooms whenever possible. The school population changed somewhat when the school district adopted a school choice policy. Most families already at Fourth Street elected to return. In addition, there were families from other parts of town who elected to send their children to Fourth Street, including, for the first time, several Mexican and

Mexican American families.This meant that I had two Hispanic children in my classroom who were new to the school and did not know the other students in my class, most of whom knew each other well.

The class had 25 students, most of whom were African American. We had two students with hearing impairments. Denise's HI was mild, and she was with us most of the day; Amy's HI was quite severe, and she was only with us for lunch and limited academic time. We had six students identified as gifted, and four as behaviorally disturbed. Of the latter, two with severe emotional problems had frequent disruptive outbursts, including screaming, crawling on the floor, and inappropriate talk (both were placed in self-contained settings, one a state mental hospital, midway through the year). The class had a collective reputation for having boundless energy, high creativity, and difficulty focusing.

What I learned from getting to know this diverse and energetic group of students was that until we were able to respect each other, we had little hope of reaching out to the broader community. Our LEADS group had read *The Dreamkeepers: Successful Teachers of African American Children*. One of the things that impressed me in the classrooms Gloria Ladson-Billings (1994) studied was a strong sense of a caring community, and the teacher's role in creating it. But in our classroom, I saw students excluding both the Hispanic students and the students with hearing impairments. Sometimes the exclusion was obvious: the students struggled so they would not be next to Amy when we lined up for recess or lunch. Amy had severe facial imperfections and could hear very little, and her speech was almost unintelligible. Further, she was only with us part of the day, so the kids didn't really get to know her. They treated her as someone with a deformity they might catch if they stood next to her. There was taunting specific to the Mexican students (e.g., "Ricardoo, you smell like doo-doo"). I was surprised and dismayed as I watched a student-written skit shared during writing workshop in which one character referred to another as "a tortilla-eating fool"; the author asked Ricardo to play the character referred to.

More often, the exclusion was more subtle. Children were not chosen for classroom projects, to read or write with, or to play with at recess. The Hispanic boys were always the last chosen for sports teams during recess. Most name-calling and taunting went on behind my back, for I made it clear immediately and repeatedly each time one of the above situations occurred that this was unacceptable behavior. It disturbed me that the worst offenders were those who usually led class discussions and took responsible class roles; they now led the teasing, name-calling, and exclusion.

The children reacted differently to the discrimination. While José tended to withdraw, Ricardo acted as if he were oblivious to the exclusion and insults. He did play the part of "the tortilla-eating fool" in the play. He coped by going along, being good-natured, not complaining. The other students interacted with him more, but continued the putdowns. It was hard for me to determine what may have been acceptable within the norms of that particular African American community, but since these putdowns always referred to his ethnicity, I saw them as unacceptable. Evidently, José did, too. Finally, he came to me—the only time all year that this shy young man initiated a personal conversation with me. He told me that the kids were picking on him and calling him names.

TEACHING TOLERANCE

I realized we had to address the problem directly, in the classroom. Discussing a children's book about how one kind of animal didn't like another kind wasn't going to cut it. I read a very helpful resource, *Holocaust History for Hope, Healing, and Humanity*, written by elementary teacher Kristine CasaBianca (1995). It is a teaching unit about respecting difference, exactly what I wanted to address. After reading her work, I wrote objectives for the behaviors I hoped would emerge as our class addressed prejudice versus understanding and acceptance:

- Showing respect for ourselves and others
- Speaking out when we see bullying, scapegoating, and other mean behavior
- Standing up for what we know is right, even when others do not, and
- Believing that each person is special, but that people are also a lot alike

I envisioned our work in concentric circles of understanding, beginning with history and circling in to the specifics of our classroom community (see Figure 2.1).

Drawing from Literature

Students read from a wide variety of sources, including the basal anthology, my extensive classroom library, and the school library. A unit on biography in our basal provided the entry point for studying prejudice. We began in February, Black History Month, with immersion in biographies. We read the basal selections in common, and had lively discussions

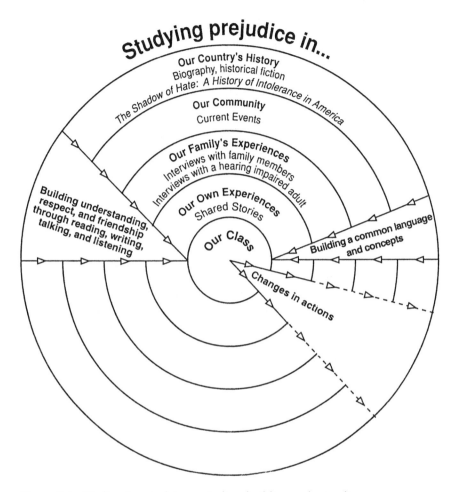

Figure 2.1. Circling in—studying prejudice, building understanding.

about the obstacles Marian Anderson encountered in entertainment and Roberto Clemente in baseball. I read picture books including *Teammates* (Golenbock, 1990), *Cheyenne Again* (Bunting, 1995), and *Smokey Night* (Bunting, 1994), chapters from collections, and biographies. The students were fascinated by the lives of Jackie Robinson, Mae Jemison, Martin Luther King, and Albert Einstein (who was rejected as "weird" by his peers and dropped out of school). In addition, each child read a biography of an African American who had made an important contribution to America (this was coupled with a study of the states), providing many examples of prejudice and overcoming discrimination for discussion. I also read

aloud historical fiction, including *Letters from Rifka* (Hesse, 1994), who
was discriminated against as an immigrant, a female, and a Jew; *Reflections
of a Black Cowboy* (Miller, 1991–92); and *They Led the Way* (Johnston, 1973),
an anthology of important women in America, which many boys as well
as girls read after I read parts. I read *The Friendship* (Taylor, 1987), which
specifically explores verbal racial insults, hoping to address the name-
calling among classmates. Overall, the students were quick to recognize
the injustices they found in these biographical and fictionalized life stories,
and to share their feelings of outrage. But the challenge remained for me
to bring this awareness into the everyday interactions of our classroom
lives.

Building a Common Language

After building this shared base of knowledge, I created a list of words
that we would need to understand in order to go into further depth:
*discriminate, prejudice, bigotry, sexism, biased, racist, attacker, racism, intoler-
ance, stereotype,* and *victim.* "We're going to study prejudice," I explained.
"Here are some of the vocabulary words we're going to be using as we
study it. Next week, these will also be our spelling words." I distributed
college "blue books" for them to use as notebooks during the study, and
asked them to find dictionary definitions of each word. The next day, we
read and discussed the varying definitions they had found in different
dictionaries. The next task was to try to understand why people discriminate. These 9- and 10-year-old students generated the following list:

> The way they were raised
> Fear
> Don't like people who are different
> Religion
> Jealousy
> To feel powerful
> Low self-esteem

I doubted any group of adults could have developed a more honest
or insightful list. The students were deeply involved in this study, often
asking, "Are we going to talk about prejudice today?" They began bringing in examples of prejudice from the local newspaper, which we then
discussed. They talked for days about the police shooting of a young
African American man who had been running naked through the streets.
They talked about the injustice of killing someone who "wasn't hurting
anyone."

Next we revisited books we had read during the year, including many of the biographies and historical fiction. Students discussed issues from the books and decided what each was an example of. Throughout the rest of the study, we added these people's names to the wall chart by the appropriate vocabulary words. With the more holistic understanding we had from our wide reading, and the more specific definitions from the vocabulary discussion, we had the foundation we needed to begin moving closer to home.

The Shadow of Hate

A resource I found particularly helpful was *The Shadow of Hate: A History of Intolerance in America* (Guggenheim, 1995). This powerful video is distributed free by the Southern Poverty Law Center, along with accompanying materials for teachers and texts for older students. I was worried that the video might be too violent (especially the lynchings), too upsetting in its entirety, but I wanted my students to get a sense of the many different groups who have faced discrimination in our country. This was particularly important since it was primarily African American students who were leading the name-calling and exclusion in our classroom; they and their families had undoubtedly been the victims of discrimination, but they needed to understand that they had a responsibility not to perpetuate the practice against others.

So I decided to show a few of the early segments. The students were visibly and vocally upset by the terrible injustices they witnessed. They asked to see the whole video; I put them off, but they begged for several days until I agreed. We learned both history and heartache as we watched how from the beginning of our country, different groups were derided and denied rights: Quakers, Native Americans, Baptists, Irish Catholics, African Americans, Japanese Americans, Chinese Americans, Mexican Americans, and Jews. We saw instances when prejudice and hatred were backed by wealth and/or power: Henry Ford, Theodore Bilbo, the KKK, David Duke, and Louis Farrakhan.

Perhaps the segment that did the most in terms of moving us toward the center of the circle—our classroom community—was the story of Felix Longoria. A young soldier from Texas, this Mexican American man was killed in battle in 1945. His hometown mortuary refused to hold his chapel service, "because the whites would not like it." The injustice became a national issue, and Longoria was eventually buried with full military honors at Arlington National Cemetery.

How could an American soldier be treated this way? The students were outraged. "That could have been somebody in Ricardo's family!"

one of the class leaders sputtered—a student who had been guilty of treating Ricardo unkindly. We were getting closer to our own lives, but we still hadn't talked about ourselves. It was easier for the kids to address prejudice in other people.

Interviewing Family Members

Each student asked some adult in his or her family if they'd ever been discriminated against. Almost all the students came back brimming with stories that they or the family member had written in their notebooks. Students read or told the stories during sharing time, discussed incidents, and added these family members' names to the vocabulary list as further examples of racism, sexism, and so forth.

Andrew wrote about his dad's experience with stereotyping of African American men:

> My dad works two jobs, on his way to the second job, he was victim of racial discrimination. My dad did not drive that day. My mother dropped him off so she could go back to work. He decided to smoke before he went to work because you couldn't smoke in the building. He was standing near a tree smoking and the police were called because he was standing in the bank parking lot. He was treated rude and like a criminal because of the color of his skin.

Most of the adults wrote about discrimination in their workplaces. Several told of missing out on opportunities for advancement that went to "some young college kid." Their age, experience, or loyalty to the company didn't seem to count. The students decided this was "ageism," which we added to our vocabulary list.

Donald's mom was one of 16 children in her family. She wrote in his notebook:

> When growing up I, along with all of my sisters, was forced to do chores around the house. While my brothers were forced to do chores outside the house. The reason I felt discriminated against was because my parents felt that simply because I was a female I should have to cook, do dishes, sweep, mop, vacuum, do laundry, etc.

My students definitely thought this was unfair!

Denise, who has a hearing impairment but manages well with a combination of a hearing aid, lip reading, and understandable speech, is the only hearing person in her family. She shared the following story:

> My mom could not order the food through the speaker at McDonalds. So she went through the drive in and tried to order the food through writing on a piece of paper. But the person at the window would not take the order. That person told my mom to go inside of McDonalds and order the food.

Her classmates could not believe the injustice. At that age, there is no more inalienable right than drive-through service at McDonald's. None of their reading had given them any insight on what it might be like to grow up in a deaf family. Denise's story really opened their eyes to discrimination against people with physical differences.

At this point, after consulting with the teacher of HI students in our building, we asked Matthew to speak with us. He was a university student, himself deaf, who volunteered regularly in the HI classroom. He signed, so he brought an interpreter. The kids generated questions ahead of time, then interviewed him about what it was like growing up as a deaf person. He told how important his mom was in his development, how she had learned to sign so they could communicate and had made him feel he could do anything. His father never learned to sign. His parents divorced when he was young, and he rarely saw his father.

More than his handicapping condition, many of my students saw someone like themselves, someone whose father's absence had hurt and confused him. They asked how it made him feel that his dad had not been very involved in his life. Nick assured him, "We're a lot like you—some of us—our dad treats us the same way." After that visit, I felt like we had reached one of our objectives: Believing that each person is special, but that people are also a lot alike.

Personal Stories

Following the sharing of adult stories, I told the students, "I want you to think about things that have happened to you, in your life. Go home, think about the assignment, then write your own experiences in your notebook."

Not everyone wrote, but as those who did shared their stories, others remembered incidents that they then told. For example, Chaundra talked about how she felt about being called a "tomboy," and pressures to be more "girlish." Donald wrote, "When I went to get my haircut they said to me, 'We don't do white hair,' and he was giving a person the cut I wanted!" Damien, who had moved from California, recounted an incident at the YMCA in his hometown:

> When I took swimming lessons I was in the front of the swimming line. I had to get in the back of the line, and so did all the other black kids. I never got as much help as the white people.

And Denise wrote, "Lots of times people think I'm dumb and stupid because I can't hear good. They laugh at the way I talk."

The Hispanic students didn't write anything. I don't think they could take that risk; I suspect they were afraid anything they said would be the basis for more teasing. In fact, no one wrote or spoke about anything that had happened in the class. Their silence illustrated that our wonderful discussions remained somewhat removed; we had begun to deal with our own lives, but not yet with our own prejudices.

Connecting with Grace

The picture book *Amazing Grace* by Mary Hoffman (1991) led us into greater awareness and problem-solving about our own classroom. Grace, who loves stories and spends hours acting them out, wants to be Peter Pan in her class play. One classmate tells her she can't because Peter is a boy; another tells her she can't because Peter Pan isn't black. Grace's grandmother, from Trinidad, takes her to the theater to see Romeo and Juliet, starring a black ballerina. Grace is inspired, wins the audition, and delights everyone with her portrayal.

After reading the story, we discussed how Grace's classmates discriminated against her. Students quickly cited specific examples of racist and sexist comments to Grace. Then I asked, "Does anything like this ever happen in our class?" Immediately students began recounting the very incidents that I had been observing: not wanting to line up near people, name-calling, teasing; interestingly, they did not mention the scene in the play that had bothered me so much. They began in a safe place, talking about incidents in general terms without naming names or accusing each other (or admitting guilt). As the trust level built, I asked the students to categorize different groups in our classroom. They listed 13 groups: handicapped, boys, racially mixed, hearing-impaired, Hispanic, Asian American, speech-impaired, African American, European American, Jewish, girls, kids, and grown-ups.

"How are we going to change the way we act in this classroom?" I asked. They began listing what not to do: no name-calling, no picking on people. I wanted positive actions, so I rephrased my question: "What are some positive guidelines to help us change the way we treat each other?"

The discussion was open and lively. The most common suggestion was, "Treat others the way you want to be treated." One fascinating thing I learned was that often students really had no idea when something they said hurt another person's feelings. These were not mean kids. One student said during the discussion, "Jeremy used to always tease me, but after I told him that it made me feel bad, he quit doing it." Our reading, interviewing, writing, and discussing had raised their awareness considerably, but they still needed help from their classmates to know what was hurtful or offensive. So the final list we posted included actions for everyone, the teased as well as the teasers:

Treat others the way you want to be treated.
When you pick on somebody you should think about the other person's feelings first.
Think before saying anything.
Share your feelings.
Tell them it hurts your feelings.
Put a note on their desk to remind them to be kind.

THE HEART OF THE CIRCLE: FROM TOLERANCE TO FRIENDSHIP

As every teacher knows, from that moment forward my students were perfect—no unkind words, no playground scuffles, no hurt feelings.

Of course that was not the case. But there was a very real difference in the way students treated one another. I noticed; the students noticed; parents even noticed. At parent conferences several weeks later, unsolicited, one black parent and one white parent (whose child had been teased considerably less about his weight since our discussions) told me how much they appreciated the study. They said that their children were really more aware of the issues now, and the adults appreciated the opportunity to talk with their children about such concerns at home, to be resources for their child's schoolwork.

The Hispanic students began to be sought after on teams, a combination of our talks and their realization that José was a really good ballplayer. Friendships began to develop among Ricardo and José and other boys in the class. Students became more tolerant of Amy, but because she moved away, there was no opportunity for deeper understanding or friendship. Denise, however, became close friends with Sherrie and some of the other girls, including sleepovers at one another's houses. The putdowns I had heard during games earlier in the year were less frequent, and I now heard,

"That's okay, you'll get it next time." There was also more inclusiveness in classroom group work. Students developed an awareness of individual strengths and began to value different contributions in group work. The problem with lining up totally disappeared.

But it was the ballet that really brought everyone together. We participated in the New York City Ballet outreach program, Storytelling Through Dance. Students write, choreograph, and perform their own numbers. After determining the tasks before and during the performance, students applied for jobs. We immersed ourselves in reading and writing *pourquoi* tales, watching ballet and other performances on video, and studying dance with a local dance teacher. After each student read his or her tale, the class discussed them all and then chose two to perform. One of their criteria was that the story had to have many roles so that every student in the class could be included. The group worked as a real team. Excellent dancers helped those who were rhythmically challenged. The choreography was varied and intricate; they worked very hard to polish the synchronization.

We performed to a packed lunchroom of the whole school, parents, and community members. The first number was "How the Stars Got in the Sky," choreographed to John Williams's "Olympic Fanfare." They performed beautifully, and received enthusiastic applause from the audience. But they really brought the house down with "How Zebras Got Their Stripes." The students had chosen music by Michael Jackson, and had studied choreography from *Thriller* and *West Side Story*. Ricardo emerged as a leader with a real dramatic sense; he did much of the choreography as well as the dancing. All the students seemed to respect his ability and to respond well to his leadership. As this familiar and well-loved music boomed out, my students moved across the stage as one body, moonwalking, sliding, snapping their fingers, and delighting the audience, adults and children alike.

We couldn't have done this at the beginning of the year. I don't think we could have done it at all if we hadn't really examined our prejudices, placed them in a broader historical perspective of discrimination and its devastating effects, and made specific, articulated plans to treat each other the way we wanted to be treated. My hope is that all my students will take this developing awareness of themselves and understanding of others with them as they move into the widening circles of the world outside of school. If they follow their own suggestions, perhaps the work we've done will make a difference not only for them, but for all they meet through their life ballets. Perhaps they will choreograph parts for everyone: not only for Grace, but for Denise and Amy, for José and Ricardo, and for others they meet who dance different dances.

REFERENCES

Bunting, E. (1994). *Smokey night*. San Diego: Harcourt Brace.

Bunting, E. (1995). *Cheyenne again*. New York: Clarion Books.

CasaBianca, K. A. (1995). *Holocaust history for hope, healing, and humanity*. Published by the author, 5230 North Grey Mountain Trail, Tucson, AZ, 85715.

Golenbock, P. (1990). *Teammates*. San Diego: Harcourt Brace Jovanovich.

Guggenheim, C. (1995). *The shadow of hate: A history of intolerance in America* (videotape). Montgomery, AL: Southern Poverty Law Center.

Hesse, K. (1994). *Letters from Rifka*. New York: H. Holt.

Hoffman, M. (1991). *Amazing Grace*. New York: Dial Books.

Johnston, J. (1973). *They led the way: 14 American women*. New York: Scholastic.

Ladson-Billings, G. (1994). *The Dreamkeepers: Successful teachers of African American children*. San Francisco: Jossey-Bass.

Lewis, B. A. (1991). *The kid's guide to social action: How to solve the social problems you choose—and turn creative thinking into positive action*. Minneapolis: Free Spirit Publications.

Miller, R. (1991–92). *Reflections of a black cowboy*. Englewood Cliffs, NJ: Silver Burdett Press.

Taylor, M. (1987). *The friendship*. New York: Dial Books for Young Readers.

Rethinking schools: An urban educational journal (various years).

Teaching Tolerance (various years).

CHAPTER 3

Addressing Social Justice in Class Meetings: Can We Choose Our Battles?

Tricia Taylor

THE FIRST TIME SOMEONE ASKED ME to explain what social justice meant to me, I was interviewing for a position with a community development project in Washington, D.C. "It all comes down to resources," I told the interviewer. "Social justice means equalizing—or coming as close as possible to equalizing—the access that each group of people in our society has to resources. And those resources could be a number of things," I elaborated, "money, transportation, food, land, education."

I had anticipated such a question. The job announcement called for an applicant committed to social justice issues. For the past two years, I had been working with low-income residents and homeless people in Washington, D.C. through various programs, most of which pertained specifically to urban land and food distribution issues. But when the interviewer asked which resource I thought was the most important, I did not answer with money, food, or land, but with education.

Motivated by the desire to "equalize the resources," I moved to Athens to get my teaching certification and master's degree in middle school education at the University of Georgia. Still motivated by social justice and equity, I developed a broader, more encompassing view of education as a critical element in social change. I developed a belief that schools could teach young people to be critical and active citizens in our society and help them be more tolerant of those who have different opinions. I searched for literature that addressed such concepts and sought out people who believed in them. I found both when I joined Literacy Education for a Democratic Society (LEADS).

As a young European American woman pondering my role in society and in schools, I was particularly struck by Edelsky's (1994) challenge to educate for the sake of democracy. She explained that "education for bringing about democracy would aim at helping put an end to the systems of domination that create the condition we have now—a condition of decidedly unequal influence over who gets what" (p. 253). I was invigorated by Edelsky's words. I agreed that our society was saturated with systems of domination and privilege, yet I questioned how to actually educate for democracy, since "we surely don't have one now" (p. 253). It seemed reasonable that if we are to teach for democracy, then we should teach in a democratic manner. As John Dewey (1916) argued, people need to experience a democracy in order to know how to function within it and visualize where it may lead.

The words of educators and philosophers made democratic teaching sound so right. But as Dewey himself might have recommended, I needed to *experience* a democratic classroom, one in which students made meaningful decisions and shared different opinions openly. To better understand democratic teaching, I volunteered with two LEADS members and teachers, Suzanne McCotter and Sara Glickman. It was my first tangible vision of democratic teaching. I saw the kind of teaching and learning that I wanted going on in my classroom, particularly their team meetings, which were tailored after town meetings (see Chapter 8).

My regular student teaching assignment, however, was not in Suzanne's or Sara's classroom. It was with 22 4th graders at a school about 20 miles away from Athens in a rural town—one traffic light, a gas station, a video store, and a few other essentials. Each day, I conducted class meetings, which I adapted from Suzanne and Sara's team meeting format. The meetings were not meant to replace student input throughout the rest of the day. Rather, they were a guaranteed time of day when students could voice their opinions, suggest and talk about change, and experience democracy in action.

During the class meetings, my students had several discussions about discrimination, stereotyping, and fairness. Students often spoke with much insight and empathy about certain social justice issues, such as race relations, insisting that all people should be treated equally. However, the students did not always apply the same rules to other groups who are discriminated against in our society. Even more disturbing was the lack of support that I experienced in the university setting, where many of my colleagues choose to either ignore or exclude particular social justice issues. Difficult questions grew out of the daily meetings, questions about the complexities and inconsistencies behind encouraging students to address social justice on some fronts, and deliberately silencing them on others.

ADDRESSING SOCIAL JUSTICE IN CLASS MEETINGS

One of the first class meetings centered around an incident that occurred after a local basketball game. According to the newspaper, a Black man was accused of drawing a large knife and a White man was accused of pointing a gun at another person. The students brought the incident up during the Community Problems and Solutions discussion at our meeting. James explained from his perspective, "The Black team won, so the White team made fun of them. Then someone on the White team pulled a gun." His comment sparked a long discussion. More students gave their interpretations of what happened at the game.

"They [the "White team"] are just prejudiced," said Mike, a White student in the class. James, a Black student, quickly replied that he thought the "White team" would have ridiculed the other team regardless of color.

"Do you think they were mad because they lost that game and used color as an excuse?" I asked the class. James and the majority of the class agreed. James also added that not all of the people on the White team were "mean." After all, only one person pulled a gun and only a handful of people shouted names, he explained.

"Okay, so sometimes we judge a whole group of people on what a few of those people do?" I asked in an attempt to clarify what James had just said. The students offered solutions, recommending that the people at the game should have just walked away or said something like, "We won fair and square. Leave us alone."

I was impressed with the students' understanding of discrimination and stereotypes. Although there was a confrontation between people of two different races, the students saw that not all members of either group were involved; not all of the White people or all of the Black people were "mean." For our vocabulary list that week, I included terms such as *discrimination, stereotype,* and *culture* so that the class would have words for the concepts we were referring to in our meetings. Other words pertained to the actual meeting, such as *agenda, format,* and *facilitator.*

In addition to incidents the students brought to class meetings, I used literature to help facilitate discussion about particular issues. I asked the students to write down topic suggestions for our meetings. They were particularly interested in issues of fairness; other topics included "problems in the room," "friends in the school," "how Kim treats Susi and Mandy better than us," "teacher's pet," "people being mean to you," and "back stabbing." Our book list included Patricia Polacco's (1992) *Chicken Sunday*, Eve Bunting's (1994) *Smokey Night*, Dr. Seuss's (1961) *The Sneetches, and Other Stories*, Rebecca Jones's (1991) *Matthew and Tilly*, and Jacqueline Martin's (1992) *Good Times on Grandfather Mountain*, among others. The students' regular classroom teacher and teachers from previous years had already shared many books on social issues with the students, so we referred easily to different books or characters to examine how others may face problems and formulate solutions.

For one meeting, I decided to use "The Sneetches," a story about creatures that judge each other based on whether or not they have stars on their bellies. After I read the book, I asked the students: "Do you think Dr. Seuss had anyone in mind when he wrote this book? Who are the Sneetches?"

"Us," answered one student.

"Blacks and Whites," said another.

"Does it have to be Black and White people?" I asked.

That question prompted the class to generate a list of things that we judge people on, including: who they hang with, where they live, if their parents are divorced, how they walk, clumsiness, skin color, clothes, accent, religion, looks, intelligence, hair color, customs, income level, sports ability, and even the size and shape of ears. Obviously, these 4th graders understood what I was talking about, and their experiences were personal. A girl whose parents were divorced listed "divorce" as a characteristic people are judged on. One of the highest achievers in class said, "intelligence," while another, less popular student added "clumsy and dumb."

With only five minutes remaining, I asked the students for possible solutions to problems that arise when we judge people based on these attributes. The only one to speak up was Mark, who very matter-of-factly called out, "Don't do it!" My sentiments exactly, I thought. I wished it were really that simple. I transcribed our list onto poster board so that we would not forget.

The Sneetches meeting, which is how I came to refer to it with my class, helped set a foundation for further discussion. More importantly, my students knew that discrimination reached far beyond the color of one's skin, understood what I meant about judging people unfairly, and offered at least one solution: "Don't do it."

CHOOSING OUR BATTLES

During my student teaching, each student chose an author to study from a class list of favorites that we had been forming. One student, Sandra, excitedly chose her favorite author. Soon after Sandra read a biographical sketch about the male author she had chosen, she approached me and read what he had written. His sketch said, "I live in New York City . . . with my boyfriend and our two cats . . . in our apartment, which is about the size of a walk-in closet."

Sandra immediately wanted to know if her author was gay. I told her that I could not guarantee it, but he probably was. Another girl added that it would have been worse if the author had been a girl. "Why would it have been worse?" I asked her, but both of the girls just stared at me. The subject was dropped for a few days, and the uneasiness of their stares left my mind. I casually mentioned the scenario to a professor of mine, who only commented that this experience might offer the students a positive image of homosexuality. I had not yet caught on to how volatile the subject of homosexuality could be.

When it was time for Sandra to present her author to the whole class, she read the "I live with my boyfriend" quote. Others in the class asked her what she thought about it. Sandra shrugged her shoulders, smiled, and said, "This doesn't mean that we can't read his books, does it?" I was encouraged by the potential of my students learning of a gay author whom they liked, in hopes that it could help break down some stereotypes. Earlier that week Sandra had read the class a book by her author, and it received high ratings. But her classmates did not respond to Sandra's question. Not wanting to impose my opinion and thinking that the students needed time to process Sandra's question, I suggested that we could discuss the topic during a class meeting.

I sensed that my students might have been somewhat homophobic. I did not, however, know that what I thought could have been a meaningful lesson in social justice was actually one of the biggest risks I could have taken, one that could have potentially ruined my student teaching in this conservative rural area. Although I did not bring up the topic of homosexuality, I certainly did not squelch it. In fact, my classroom was set up so that we could have a designated time to address it. On several occasions, I had allowed my students to discuss their feelings regarding race and gender. The students' regular teacher had also discussed with them such topics as interracial marriage and racism when they arose in the literature the class was reading. Refusing to allow homosexuality to be mentioned would have contradicted my previous statements about class meetings.

Shortly after this incident, I shared my story with two fellow student teachers who I had assumed would think nothing of it. I was wrong. Although they agreed that homophobia was a form of discrimination, I could tell from the tone of their voices that they thought I was treading on thin ice. Admittedly, I was getting a little nervous about our next class meeting. At least two students had already asked me if we could talk about "that gay author."

As soon as we reached Community Problems and Solutions, Ellen's hand shot up. "Can we talk about the gay thing?"

"Someone has to address the subject," I said. "What is your concern?"

Kris volunteered. "Does anyone in here not have a problem with it?" I was the only one to raise my hand.

Later, when a colleague asked me if I thought it was right to reveal my beliefs by raising my hand, I told her that it was not a studied decision. I raised my hand as easily as if someone had asked me if I thought racism was wrong, or sexism unjust. But immediately after I raised my hand that day, in effect saying that I had no problem with homosexuality, I knew from the wide eyes that I had done something not many of my students had ever experienced. I had defended homosexuality.

As soon as I raised my hand, Kris pushed her seat away from where I was standing. "Ms. Taylor, you aren't . . . are you?"

"No, I'm not gay, but if I were?" I asked.

"If you were, I'd leave this classroom," said James.

By now, I could feel my heart pounding. I looked to the back of the room. My lead teacher was sitting at her desk, quietly working with her head down. I told the students, "I answered your question, but I really don't think I needed to." But I knew in my heart that I *had* needed to answer. It was not just because they were 4th graders and would not understand the principle that a person's sexual orientation is private. I needed them to know that I was not gay for the sake of my own survival during student teaching. Although I was ready to stand by my beliefs if asked, I was not in a good position for martyrdom. I was an unmarried woman in her mid-twenties. To refuse comment would have been equivalent to saying I was gay. In the eyes of my students, it was bad enough that I was "homofriendly."

In an attempt to bring the conversation back to the topic and away from me, I asked, "Does it matter if an author is gay?"

Sandra, who had posed a similar question the day before, quickly responded, "God created Adam and Eve, not Adam and Adam or Eve and Eve." The conversation continued along the same vein. I suggested that we realize that different people have different religions. Some people have never heard of Christianity. Then I reminded the students that at one time some people thought it was wrong to read a book written by a Black person or a woman.

"But they were just wrong," insisted Kris. "It doesn't matter what color you are." She pointed to her crayons, telling me that each was a different color, but each still a crayon.

"But it's okay to judge someone on whether or not they are gay?" I asked. The answer was disapproving looks.

I told the class that I would act as a facilitator if they wanted to continue discussing the subject, but I felt uncomfortable with the direction of the conversation. "I think you are all trying to figure out why I think it's okay to be gay, rather than discuss the issue." The conversation soon ended.

For the remainder of the meeting, I read *The Story of Ruby Bridges* by Robert Coles (1995), a book about a girl who fought for her right to go to a newly integrated school despite protests from White community members who did not want to send their children to a school with Black students. I wondered if the students made any connections. In closing, I brought out the list we had generated from our Sneetches meeting. "Remember this?" I asked as I showed them the list. "We need to think about why we are judging people." I admitted to them that I felt very uncomfortable being the only one in the group with a different opinion. In the future, I wanted us to work harder at trying to discuss difficult issues in ways that did not alienate those with different opinions from ours. "This is a skill that you will use forever," I said. "Many adults are not able to talk about ideas if they have different opinions."

I chose not to tell my story to my university class, 19 students in a special master's program for students with non-education undergraduate degrees. We took almost every class together, which gave us ample opportunities to debate issues and learn about one another's teaching philosophies. Although predominately female, and completely White and middle-class, the cohort was a mixture of conservatives, moderates, and liberals. Few people used these labels to describe themselves, but I considered myself more liberal than most in my class. I already had the reputation for, as one of my classmates put it, "throwing a wrench into everything."

I chose not to share my story about the gay author because I did not want to have to defend myself again. The sting from my last discussion about homosexuality still resonated. We already had enough battles in our classes over less controversial issues relating, for example, to the merits of traditional versus more progressive ways of teaching. Weeks later, however, someone to whom I had told the story "volunteered" me to share. I agreed, thinking that university students would not be as harsh as 4th graders. I was wrong. Indeed, what I had told my students proved prophetic; these educated adults were not able to talk about their different opinions, at least on this topic. Again, the conversation turned, this time from how should we as teachers address homosexuality to whether what I let happen was right or wrong.

As one of my classmates noted, we could have divided the room in half between those who accepted homosexuality and those who did not. Some classmates, who under normal circumstances were openly accepting of homosexuality, sat quietly. Unfortunately for me, the classmates who did not voiced their opinions the strongest and most derisively. I was told that homosexuality was a question of morality and should not be talked about in schools. I tried the same logic I used with my 4th graders: "Remember, there was a time when some people thought it immoral for women to go to work, or for a White person to use the same toilet as a Black person." They defended the morality stance with religion, saying that homosexuality was considered by many to be anti-Christian and should therefore not be mentioned in schools. My professor only spoke to announce break time when we finished.

There were some mild attempts at understanding. "I don't agree with the lifestyle, but since I'm involved in theater, I know a lot of gay people and they are very nice," one woman said. Another classmate added that if a book was good, then it did not matter to her who wrote it, even if the person was a child molester. Later, she retracted that statement, realizing that she had likened a homosexual to a child molester, but her comment illustrates the tone that day.

At our next class session, residue from our previous meeting permeated the room, and I felt the tension as soon as I walked through the door. My classmates knew that the previous week's discussion had disturbed me. At the break I rushed out of the classroom to avoid getting upset in front of everyone. A couple of sympathetic classmates followed me to offer support, and when I returned to the room after the break, my face was still red and drained.

Despite the tension, the final presentations that following week ran routinely. Two of them, however, stood out in my mind. One classmate shared a children's book he had written about a young character who questions if there will ever be a day when people are not judged by their personal traits, such as color or learning ability. Another classmate used an analogy between the permeable membrane of a cell and the walls of her own life to illustrate that people continually move in and out of different groups throughout their lives. The cell circles, I concluded, also represented our cohort, which came together in the interest of education, but separated over philosophies, religions, and homosexuality.

I knew what it felt like to stand outside of someone else's circle. Because I had accepted homosexuality, I felt alienated from my 4th graders and from my university class. Coupled with the alienation, I also felt misunderstood. I had tried to explain to my classmates that I had not brought up the subject of homosexuality; my students had. I had not told my students that their judgments were right or wrong; I had only asked them to think about what they based their judgments on. But my vocal classmates were adamant. They told me to refuse to discuss homosexuality.

I find that solution virtually impossible. If I tell my students that I am completely against any type of discrimination, set up a forum so that we may discuss such issues, and bring in literature that addresses discrimination, how can I then deny them the opportunity to discuss homophobia or their ideas about gay authorship? How could I as a teacher not question them? Philosophically, I do not believe that we can choose our battles in a democratic classroom. How can I say I'll discuss racism, but not homophobia? If I ignored intolerance of homosexuals, wouldn't I essentially be condoning it? As a teacher whose aim was to set up a classroom atmosphere "as if" it were a democracy, I felt an obligation to uphold the high standards of democracy, such as accepting different groups of people or at least tolerating the idea that different people have different opinions.

But the words "accepting" and "tolerating"—words educators typically use when discussing multicultural or social justice education—seem to be too passive, as if we are just putting up with people who are different from us. If we are to change the status quo, "a condition of decidedly unequal influence over who gets what" (Edelsky, p. 253), we need to include all people as full and equal participants in our society. And we need to challenge others who are unwilling to do so.

I recently viewed a videotape of Sandra's author presentation. I cringed as I watched how I was initially so undaunted by the fear of discussing homosexuality. Only a few days later, I would be dreading calls from angry parents, disapproving looks from teachers, and the alienation of my students. While none of these things happened, the fear was demoralizing. Being liberal in a conservative system is not an easy position, and it surely had set me up for a challenge. White, educated, and middle-class, I have lived a relatively privileged life. I now know what it means to be excluded. The feeling of exclusion made me want to stop participating. It was this alienation, however, that helped reaffirm my commitment to social justice education.

I could have easily remained silent during the discussions with my university classmates. I could have immediately changed the subject when

Ellen asked, "Can we talk about the gay thing?" Nobody would have blamed me for wanting to avoid a heated discussion where I was outnumbered. But in the end I chose to speak up. I was confused and apprehensive, but I knew I had to say what I felt was right and what was consistent with my philosophy of promoting a democratic classroom.

I'm a teacher now, in a new school (see Chapter 10). One of my colleagues has a poster in her room with a quote from a sermon by Lutheran pastor Martin Niemoeller during the Holocaust:

> In Germany they came first for the communists, and I didn't speak up because I wasn't a communist. They came for the Jews, and I didn't speak up because I wasn't a Jew. Then they came for the trade unionists, and I didn't speak up because I wasn't a trade unionist. Then they came for the Catholics, and I didn't speak up because I was a Protestant. Then they came for me, and by that time no one was left to speak up.

While the incident in my classroom is a drop of water compared to the tidal wave of the Holocaust, societies are formed and transformed by the accumulation of incidents where people either speak up or remain silent. Speaking up helped me understand and affirm my commitment to social justice education. The difficulty of that small act convinced me of how critical it is that we continue to define for ourselves how far, and at what cost, we as teachers are willing to go to pursue democracy and social justice.

REFERENCES

Bunting, E. (1994). *Smokey night*. San Diego: Harcourt Brace.
Coles, R. (1995). *The story of Ruby Bridges*. New York: Scholastic.
Dewey, J. (1916). *Democracy and education*. New York: Macmillan.
Edelsky, C. (1994). Education for democracy. *Language Arts, 71*, 253–257.
Jones, R. (1991). *Matthew and Tilly*. New York: Dutton.
Martin, J. (1992). *Good times on Grandfather Mountain*. New York: Orchard Books.
Polacco, P. (1992). *Chicken Sunday*. New York: Philomel Books.
Seuss, Dr. (1961). *The Sneetches, and other stories*. New York: Random House.

CHAPTER 4

Being Social Scientists: A Democratic Experience in Teacher Education

Jane West, Jill Wilmarth, Cathy Crumley, Julie Dickerson, and Melissa Francis

PICTURE OUR SOCIAL STUDIES METHODS class meeting in the curriculum library of our small liberal arts college. Clusters of two or three preservice students are gathered at tables around the room pursuing our theme, Religion in Public Schools. Cathy and Lara pore over a pile of children's books, examining them carefully, talking about how different religions are portrayed in the texts and illustrations. Jill and Julie lurk on an Internet discussion about legal issues related to religion and schools; they carry on their own debate. Melissa is next door in Jane's office telephoning politicians' headquarters to learn their views on prayer in school. Kerry, Jennifer, and Katherine discuss pamphlets they've received from national organizations like the American Library Association, the American Civil Liberties Union, and local citizens' groups involved in censorship proceedings in public schools and libraries. Jane looks on, takes notes, and moves among the groups raising questions, contributing her own ideas about how the class might proceed.

We were engaged in the real investigation of questions we negotiated as a group and identified for ourselves. We selected a focus for our inquiry that enhanced our understandings of schools and sharpened our awareness of how issues of power, culture, politics, and voice are played out in classrooms and school districts across the country. Through this investigative process, class members participated in the kind of enterprise that we will someday construct with our own elementary students.

In her challenge to language educators, Edelsky (1994) wrote, "Progressive language educators help kids become literate, but we don't necessarily make them critical" (pp. 254–255). That is just as true in teacher education. A teacher educator's role is not only to help prepare students to teach, but also to help them gain a critical perspective on schooling. In the course described here, we strove to create a democratic classroom in which all members experienced "meaningful participation in the decision-making that affects our lives" (Shannon, 1993, p. 90). Our shared decision-making about the inquiry focus and investigation, the course content, and the processes of learning all contributed to the democratic nature of our classroom.

According to Goodman (1992), all participants in an educational endeavor must share decisions, access to knowledge, and access to communicative forums. We agree, and believe that preservice teachers' voices must be better represented in professional venues. Throughout this chapter (which has been reviewed by all members of the class), our description of the inquiry is interwoven with journal entries and other commentary written by both students and instructor. Through this format we attempt to represent the perspectives of all class members and to reflect the way in which we interacted in our class.

THE INSTRUCTOR'S PERSPECTIVE

Jane describes her background, and some of the experiences and beliefs that led her to create the course:

> My comfortable middle-class childhood shielded me from much of what people become activists about. My introduction to the need for social activism came during my high school summers when I worked as a teacher's aide in the local Migrant Education program. Our task was to assist the English language and literacy learning of children among the large population of Vietnamese refugees who had come to the Mississippi Coast in the mid 1970s. That job took me into public housing developments and into parts of town I didn't know existed, into shrimp factories and onto "the docks." And it took me into the offices of doctors, lawyers, bankers, landlords, and school principals with whom our students' fam-

ilies needed to interact—only this time, I was seeing through different eyes. That experience taught me to appreciate the circumstances of people I had previously looked past, and it sparked my urge to bring about change. It also solidified my desire to teach.

Teaching has been my primary means of working for social change. I became a teacher because I wanted my life's efforts to matter for someone else. I taught in urban schools with low-income populations. Now, teaching in a small women's liberal arts college with historical Presbyterian ties, I do not experience the direct impact I did in urban public schools. However, I do believe that what I am doing matters for children in public schools, the students of my students.

In my development as a teacher educator, I'm growing uncomfortable with the writing of syllabi as a solitary act. Before I can design a course, I need to know my students, individually and collectively. I need to know what they know and believe, what's important to them, what they want to learn, and how they might best do so. My vision of what this course might be began with my social constructivist perspective and my membership in LEADS. LEADS teachers helped me further explore democratic approaches to teaching. I also read how progressive educators teach social studies; Steffey and Hood (1994), for example, provided powerful stories of teachers and students negotiating social studies curricula. Additionally, I considered my department's goal of creating the kinds of classroom experiences that we hope our students will be able to create in their own future classrooms with their students.

To those ends, Jane constructed the syllabus with $3\frac{1}{2}$ weeks of blank space at the beginning of the schedule, marked only with the words "theme study." We have since discovered new books and terminology to describe what we are doing. The work of Kathy Short and her colleagues (Short, Schroeder, Laird, Kauffman, Ferguson, & Crawford, 1996) is particularly akin to our approach. We adopted the term "inquiry" rather than theme study. Inquiry is well suited to our goals of creating a democratic classroom because of its view of curriculum as negotiated, its emphasis not only on teachers' questions but also on students', and its assumption that knowledge is not owned by the teacher and transmitted to students, but rather is the co-constructed "property" of all members of the classroom community.

INQUIRY ABOUT RELIGION IN PUBLIC SCHOOLS

With a mixture of excitement and uncertainty, we began the semester by discussing the syllabus and the possibility of conducting our own inquiry. Typical of our small college, there were nine members of the class, including the professor. Jill, Jennifer, Melissa, Lara, and Julie were midway through their teacher education coursework. Cathy and Kerry were a semester away from student teaching. Katherine, who was not planning to teach, took the course as an elective. Most class members were of traditional college age; Cathy and Lara had returned to college after having pursued other endeavors. We were all White women from middle-class Christian backgrounds, although our political and religious views varied. Among us were psychology, religious studies, art, English, sociology/anthropology, and history majors. (Our students complete programs in education in addition to their majors in other disciplines.) Many of us already knew each other; half of us had taken other classes with Jane.

Getting Started

We spent the first two weeks discussing possible themes, webbing them, constructing charts of what we already knew and what we wanted to find out, and weighing the advantages of each theme. Clearly, the first few weeks Jane had set aside for the inquiry hadn't allowed us sufficient time to "wander and wonder" (Short et al., 1996) about possible themes; we found ourselves unable to choose. We decided to continue reading about theme studies done in elementary classrooms (e.g., Lindquist, 1995; Manning, Manning, & Long, 1994; Steffey & Hood, 1994). The class narrowed the field to the three most popular suggestions: water, religion on our campus, and the importance of being different. Together we constructed webs and generated questions to investigate. Through extensive discussion, we dropped "water," and eventually merged "differences" with "religion" to create "religious diversity." Following more webbing, discussion, and question-posing, we narrowed the theme of religious diversity to "Religion in Public Schools: What Should Its Role Be?" and collaboratively generated a final web. Students selected topics, formed interest groups that addressed one or more topic, and then began their inquiries. Topics included the following:

1. *Holidays.* Which ones are celebrated? How are they celebrated?
2. *Children's literature.* How does it portray religion? What books are available?

3. *Censorship.* What groups are involved in attempting/preventing it? What are religion biases?
4. *Pledge of Allegiance.* How is "one nation under God" perceived?
5. *School prayer.* What do current political candidates say? What is being practiced?
6. *Religion in the explicit curriculum.* What is taught? What does the state curriculum guide say?

That final choice was the result of hard thought, negotiation, and compromise. Throughout the process, Jane had wanted the theme to highlight issues of social justice, but she hesitated to impose those issues, knowing that her desires would carry more weight than other class members'. However, before she could decide how to steer the class in that direction, it became evident that the most popular themes would involve those issues. Even our discussions of water included a focus on distribution and preservation of resources, economic and health issues, and how power and politics influenced who had access to clean water. Class members were already attuned to issues of social justice.

The negotiation process elicited several journal entries about the power of choice. Kerry wrote, "My ability to play an active role in the selection process gives me ownership of the theme and also illustrates to me how to give my students the ability to choose and work on areas within an inquiry that are meaningful to them." However, not everyone initially felt ownership of the theme of religion and public education. Jill, the originator of the water theme, admits her initial reluctance, explaining, "I felt a little apprehensive about the topic because it seemed like we would be doing this surface study of politically correct issues that sometimes happen in intro level classes, and I just didn't feel like going through that again!"

Cathy, too, seemed reticent about the theme. Normally a bubbly and enthusiastic learner, she sat quietly, arms folded, as the rest of the class's final theme choice became clear. Sensing her dissatisfaction, Jane urged Cathy to search for some aspect of the theme that interested her. Cathy wrote about her feelings:

> The one thing that I felt sure of was that I did not want to touch religion with a ten-foot pole! The thought of talking about religion in a school setting made me very uncomfortable. As we discussed religion as a possible theme, everyone seemed excited—except me. Jane wouldn't let us go forward, though, until everyone agreed on a theme. I compromised with a suggestion that I look at holidays and how they were celebrated in schools. Little did I know that

once I got started on the project, I would come to have a completely different view of religion and schools!

Cathy's misgivings about the theme are understandable. The country
was in the early stages of campaigns for primary elections of presidential
candidates. The religious right was an influential voice in those campaigns, and religious issues—including prayer in school—were in the
news regularly, always associated with some controversy. Several court
cases related to school prayer had also been in the news. Fundamentalist
religious groups had become active in school board matters in the district
in which Cathy lived, succeeding in getting a number of curricular initia-
tives approved. In another nearby county, Newt Gingrich's electoral district, "diversity" and "multiculturalism" in schools were becoming bad
words. Our location in the Bible Belt of the deep South means that issues
like religion in education strike very close to home for many people. Yet
neither Cathy nor Jill made her reluctance explicit, and we forged ahead
without any real discussion of the potential controversy inherent in the
theme we'd chosen.

Next we each decided whether we preferred to work with partners
or individually, identified areas of interest relating to the theme, and then
began our investigations. Melissa wrote, "I like that we all didn't have
to focus on the same topic. We learned much more by being able to choose
an area of special interest and study that." We focused on broad questions
(e.g., What opinions do people hold about the role of religion in public
schools?) and specific issues concerning the role of religion in censorship,
the celebration of holidays, and the legalities of prayer and the Pledge
of Allegiance in schools. Serendipitously, some teachers in our public
elementary partner schools had suggested that the college sponsor a forum
for discussing educational issues. The first one, held near the end of the
semester, became not only a forum for those teachers, but also a forum
in which we shared what we were learning in our inquiry.

Laying the Groundwork

One of the first journal entries we all wrote was a reflection on our own
experiences with religion in the schools we attended. These entries helped
us realize what diverse backgrounds we had despite our apparent homogeneity. Jill wrote, "In high school, the teacher in my senior government
class said that if I didn't want to say the Pledge of Allegiance, I would
have to defend why I didn't want to. I had to write a ten-page paper
about it, but then I didn't have to say it." Jennifer recalled that she was
already well aware of the issue of religion and public schools "because

when I was in high school, I was on the other side from which I am now. I didn't want to read anything that was against my religion." Cathy, returning to college after her children were grown, remembered experiences familiar to many growing up in the segregated South:

> My experience with religion in schools was reflective of white Christian Southern heritage. We had prayer every morning. We had traditional Christmas celebrations . . . I do not remember having any Jewish children in my classes, nor children of other religions or cultural backgrounds.

In response to another journal prompt, "What are my goals as a participant in this inquiry?", some class members identified goals related to specific content about religion and schools; others focused more on the kind of experience they wanted to have. Jill wrote that she saw herself "as a teacher and a learner. I want to be informed and be an informant and in the process work toward a common goal . . . of having a great product . . . I want to see how religion in schools is done now and how to bring it into my own classroom." Cathy's goal was that when she taught, she would "value each child's culture and religious background, give each child an opportunity to share information about their culture and religious holiday celebrations, stress the importance of each person and the understanding of their life and background." Melissa's goal went beyond the classroom to educating the general public as well: "I also hope to educate people about what I find out in this inquiry. I want to know specifically how and why people, students and educators, feel about the pledge and prayer being said or done during school hours or on school property."

In journals we also explored our expectations about the inquiry. Since most of us were new to this kind of enterprise, we felt a great deal of uncertainty in the beginning. Jane was just as uncertain as the students:

> I wonder what my role in all this should be. I guess it includes being a learner along with everyone else, but also ensuring that the study moves forward. I don't want my ideas about the study to supplant the students'. And I don't want to become too involved in gathering data for students' investigations since I'd like them to have that experience; I do want to provide what help I can—share what resources I have to keep them from reinventing the wheel.

Moving Forward

At first we concentrated only on the inquiry, writing frequently in journals about our experiences. After the first month, we spent one of our two weekly class periods in inquiry workshop, described in the opening of this chapter. (Alternating class meetings were spent on discussions of common texts.) In mid-semester we began planning for our presentations at the forum. Along the way we employed a wide range of research processes and a variety of data sources:

1. *Print resources* from public, college, and school libraries and book-stores—general, professional, and children's books; social studies textbooks; magazines, journals, and newspapers; pamphlets from various political and civic organizations
2. *Technological resources*—on-line catalogs; ERIC and other indexes; Internet listserves, bulletin boards, and World Wide Web sites
3. *Human resources*—teachers, principals, and district administrators; librarians and bookstore representatives; representatives of political candidates; people from organizations such as the ALA, NEA, ACLU, and Peace Corps; and friends, classmates, and family

We had many different entry points. Jennifer wrote that since she hadn't read many banned books, "I felt that it was in the best interest of the study to read [them] . . . I'm going to call school libraries in the Atlanta area and ask if any of the books on my list have been banned from their libraries, and if so, who did it." Classmates often shared information with each other, as Melissa reported: "Just this morning Cathy gave me an article from *NEA Today* . . . [and] I have some copies of information that I got from [a political science professor]. . . . [I]t deals mostly with the legal aspect of prayer in school."

Julie and Jill started with their personal web of possible resources, then made a list of some ways they could find out how school systems deal with controversy over religion in the classroom. They began with telephone interviews of school personnel. Since Jill identified herself as "phonephobic," Julie did the first interviews. They found some school representatives quite willing to talk with them, but felt that others were being less than candid. After one official told them, "There have been no specific problems that I have been made aware of," a teacher in his district reported to Julie that she'd opened her class with prayer each morning until very recently. "I didn't think of it as bringing religion into the classroom; I was just doing what was second nature to me. The only reason I stopped was because a parent from another class happened to look in on our class one day." In our next class meeting, Julie and Jill stumbled over each other's words as they explained what they'd found from these early interviews. Their amazement at the variety of viewpoints led them to search for voices from outside the education system.

Learning as We Go

As with most research, some of our original topics changed substantially; we posed new questions as we found information and constructed ideas. We also began to learn, as all researchers do, that things don't always progress as planned. For example, some of us thought the process would move more quickly. Jennifer offered one explanation for why the research was taking longer than anticipated:

> Our group continually redefines what it is that we are researching. At first we were looking on a national level trying to really grasp and understand censorship . . . When [the public] library . . . didn't have many of the books I was looking for, [that] got me thinking on a local level. Are there certain communities that would have more of a problem with certain books than others, and who is predominantly in those communities?

Several of us worried when we didn't get responses from people we contacted. Kerry wrote that "many organizations aren't very organized and sometimes aren't that open and receptive to the public" after a pair of particularly frustrating attempts to get information for her group's study of the role of religion in censorship. She tried to visit the headquarters of a local organization often involved in advocating censorship of literature in schools. She discovered after spending a morning searching that the address on their letterhead was incorrect. She found that the local authorities had no record of such an organization. Kerry began to suspect that "this was a bogus, phony thing." When she finally reached the organization's headquarters by phone, she was suspiciously received, and the representative refused to discuss the issue with her or send any information. Kerry had initially learned of the group's existence through its pamphlet warning of children "being exposed to certain books" and of the "liberal" policies of the American Library Association. Ironically, Kerry reported that when she called the ALA for their position statement on censorship, she was told to "look it up."

Cathy, too, encountered reluctance when she called an elementary school near her home to request an interview about how holidays were celebrated in this culturally diverse school. The principal told her she needed the superintendent's written approval. Surprised at such a request, the superintendent's office nevertheless faxed its okay to the school. Two weeks and three unreturned phone calls later, Cathy became angry. She wrote a letter to the school board from her perspective as a twenty-year taxpaying resident whose children had attended schools in that system, expressing her frustrations with the way she, as a member of the public, had been treated. She never received a reply.

Though we sometimes had difficulty getting information, we also experienced willing cooperation. After her frustration with one school, Cathy had some good luck:

> I was extremely fortunate in finding this [educational magazine] article because I discovered that [the author] is a principal in the [Atlanta] area and was delighted to take time out of her schedule to talk with me . . . [S]he was gracious enough to make copies of the guidelines which she gives to her teachers, . . . as well as copies from her legal books concerning religion and public education.

Julie was similarly excited and surprised when a busy district curriculum director returned her call the same day. "She was very interested in our topic and proceeded to answer all my questions, and gave me lots of new ones as well."

Melissa, pursuing her questions surrounding prayer and the Pledge in schools, found presidential candidates happy to offer their views, vague though they often were. A frequent answer to her telephone requests for information was something like, "Yes, he is an ardent supporter of both prayer and the Pledge in school." Most had official statements supporting the laws currently in place. Of her telephone interviews, Melissa recalls,

> I sat on my bed in my dorm room with the list of presidential candidates in my hands and called each of their headquarters. Even though I have always had an interest in politics, this was the first time I felt like I was educating myself as a voter. I could never have imagined the excitement that comes with calling up the candidates' headquarters and asking them questions about the issues. This was such a personal way to collect information for my inquiry, and I knew that with each call I was getting more involved with this year's presidential election.

As Melissa discovered the power of being an informed citizen, Jill and Julie discovered the wealth of information on the Internet. They spent hours crowded behind Julie's overflowing desk following a discussion among law students and professors, elected officials, and teachers about prayer in school. Their room rang with shouts of "Yes! Thank you for acknowledging the conservative agenda toward the 'captive' school audience! We *need* lawyers like this guy." "Okay, when did this knucklehead speak to Christ? First he says that Jesus wants only Christians to model Jesus' behavior, then he says government shouldn't teach anything to the general public. Doesn't he realize that we're talking about public education here?" Julie and Jill realized that it is often politicians rather than educators deciding the fate of their future classrooms, and recalled Weaver's (1994) discussion of the power and agenda of the religious right on politics and education.

REPRESENTING OUR LEARNING

Our groups generated a wide array of products as a result of their investigations. Jane required that everyone construct an inquiry portfolio. Class members insisted that since their research had been collaborative, their portfolios should be as well. Other products included bibliographies and displays of children's books that had been banned and books depicting holidays or other aspects of religion; informational fliers about political candidates' views; a revised course syllabus; a list of groups involved in initiating or opposing censorship proceedings; laws relating to prayer in school and legal guidelines for teachers; a list of ideas for incorporating the study of diverse religions into the social studies curriculum; essays about religion and education; and some very polished presentations at the forum, complete with handouts and visuals.

At the forum, the 10 of us were joined by other college faculty members, public and private school teachers, and other students at the college—a group of about 25 in all. Katherine, Kerry, and Jennifer described what they had learned about the role of religious beliefs in censorship in schools, shared passages from children's books about censorship, and provided lists of previously banned books along with information they'd received from anti-censorship groups. Jill and Julie did a reader's theater performance of excerpts of the on-line discussion they'd participated in on legal issues pertaining to religion and schools. Melissa gave a talk about prayer in school and displayed charts of politicians' positions on the matter. Cathy and Lara shared a wealth of ideas they'd gathered from teachers about inclusive approaches to religious studies in the social studies curriculum, displayed a variety of children's books with religious themes or information, and provided an extensive bibliography. Audience members related their own experiences with religion in school, and teachers talked about how they approach issues of religion in their classrooms.

Attendees provided written feedback about our efforts; all declared the gathering a success and expressed interest in the possibility of holding future forums on other topics. Julie, noting the increased responsibility of presenting to others already in the field, reflected that presenting "adds another level to this research, because I am not doing this for personal reasons only." Expressing the opinion of several class members, she wrote, "This was probably my most memorable experience at [our college]. All of the hard work seemed to really be rewarded by the Forum. It was a great way to 'show off' all we had learned and a great way to include the community in our final product." Participants listened, asked questions, and took handouts.

WHEN DEMOCRATIC THEORY AND PRACTICE MEET

In taking steps toward education for democracy (Edelsky, 1994), we directed our own learning on an issue directly related to democracy and education. Having a public audience moved us toward breaking down barriers and seeing real change occur. We have new insight about being a member of a religious minority in a Southern public school classroom. We reconsidered how holidays are celebrated in public schools, and clarified our opinions about prayer, the Pledge, and teaching about "other" religions in public schools. In doing so, we have begun to recognize what Edelsky (1994) identifies as "systems of domination," to critique the status quo, and to make plans for education *for* democracy in our own classroom.

We all learned a great deal both about our theme and about schools and teaching. Julie realized "how this issue affects everyone, not just teachers and students. I have read accounts of entire communities taking sides and battling it out in school board meetings as well as in courts, so I know I may very well have to deal with this [as a teacher] myself one day." We really related what we'd learned to decisions we faced as teachers. Cathy concluded that including religion in culture studies "would add to the richness of the classroom as well as help the children to appreciate . . . how [religions] are an integral part of every culture. I would make sure that religion was discussed [throughout] the curriculum and not [just] at special holiday times." Some, like Katherine, changed our thinking about issues:

When we started this inquiry, I thought I already knew exactly how I felt about censorship and book banning . . . One thing I'm finding is that a lot of book banning happens because the adults do not expect children to make intelligent decisions on their own. I think they are really afraid that they will end up with different beliefs than their parents.

In our journals, we also reflected on the inquiry process. Cathy, originally concerned about the time and effort involved, wrote:

> I have learned that through ownership, enthusiasm is generated, a thirst for knowledge about the subject appears, and that there is no need to prompt students to do their work when they're truly interested and the project belongs to them. I know that I read this in my book, but it is in the experience that ownership takes place.

Jill identified additional values of the inquiry: "We're making multiple connections with the community, which I think is vital. We are listening to the voices of the community. . . . We are also learning what it feels like to be in a democratic classroom. We will have a real, tangible experience to draw from when we finally become teachers."

Though the course is over, our learning in the inquiry goes on. Jill and Jane presented an early version of this paper at the National Reading Conference. Cathy and Lara made a presentation on religion in children's literature for a regional professional conference. Kerry and Cathy, student-teaching in multi-age 3rd-, 4th-, and 5th-grade classrooms, helped students to conduct exciting, challenging inquiries. Kerry and Cathy found that their student teaching experience resembled what they observed in the inquiry: Religion was omitted entirely from the curriculum. Easter was celebrated with baskets of candy but no acknowledgment that it was a religious holiday.

Despite our good intentions, however, the study had its flaws. The efforts of some class members exceeded the group's expectations, while others' efforts fell short. While most class members experienced the power of learner voice and choice in enhancing motivation (Oldfather & Dahl, 1994), apparently some did not. One group had trouble getting their inquiry moving; one member reported in her self-evaluation that the group hadn't done its best. And while students constructed portfolios to represent their learning and evaluated themselves, Jane still determined the final grades, rather than having students grade themselves.

Another flaw occurred to us as we worked on this chapter. In our attempts to include as many perspectives as possible, we failed to hear the most important voices—the children's. Representing children's perspectives in educational research represents a shift toward attention to those least powerful members of the education community (LeCompte &

Preissle, 1992) and has the potential of facilitating understandings of life in schools otherwise inaccessible to researchers and even to teachers. Had we included children in our inquiry, we might have learned what it feels like to be the sole Jewish child in a classroom of Protestants, or what 5th graders think about censorship based on religious beliefs. These perspectives would have greatly enriched our study.

On the other hand, we *were* social scientists for that semester. We engaged in the intellectual activity of sociologists, anthropologists, political scientists, economists, historians, psychologists, and especially educators. Though we did not have the usual single-classroom field experience, we visited numerous classrooms and interviewed not only teachers, but also principals, curriculum supervisors, superintendents and assistant superintendents, and public and school librarians, as well as lawyers, political figures and their spokespersons, professional organizations such as the American Library Association, and activist groups such as the American Civil Liberties Union and the American Family Association. We consulted professional journals in education, newspapers, pamphlets and position statements published by various organizations, elementary social studies textbooks, children's literature, popular magazines, and books. We learned to conduct ERIC searches, and we used the Internet for posting queries on listserves, searching the World Wide Web, and participating in discussion groups. We experienced meaningful learning about social studies education in a way that has changed our ideas about teaching.

LESSONS FOR DEMOCRATIC TEACHER EDUCATION

All Jane's courses now address issues of social justice in some way. Readings and discussions address marginalized groups and the least powerful members of the education community. She and her students continually work to foreground issues of democracy, to understand the rights of learners to shape their own educations, to experience the power of voice, and to do all this more purposefully. Each semester, the students have more choices about how they will learn and be evaluated. Jane is learning from her students that she must make these issues and actions explicit if they are to construct similar experiences with their students. Still, she struggles with her role in democratizing teacher education:

> I feel a tension between wanting my students to see teaching as a political act and wanting them to find their own ways into teaching. I must guard against engendering what Gordon Pradl (1996)

described as "the true believer," who shares my perspective simply because I am the teacher. My dilemma is this: Part of education for democracy is the right to set one's own agenda. I want to follow my students' leads, yet I can't just wait for social/political issues to come up; I must *create* ways for that to happen. I hold my breath against the day when a class wants to study "teddy bears." Unlikely, but possible. More likely, a group of students might overlook the social/political aspects of a chosen theme. I can tell students, "I think it's really important to address these kinds of issues. What do you think? How might we do this?" Yet some students are unlikely to disagree openly with something their teacher obviously values. To what degree is my direction coercive or controlling, and to what degree is it a legitimate function of a teacher? To what degree is a student's resistance to social/political issues an indicator of the quality of her work (i.e., how does it influence her grade)? When does a professor's focus on the study of democratic issues stop being democratic?

REFERENCES

Edelsky, C. (1994). Education for democracy. *Language Arts, 71*, 252–257.

Goodman, J. (1992). *Elementary schooling for critical democracy.* Albany: State University of New York Press.

LeCompte, M. D., & Preissle, J. (1992). Toward an ethnology of student life in schools and classrooms: Synthesizing the qualitative research tradition. In M. D. LeCompte & W. L. Millroy (Eds.), *The handbook of qualitative research in education* (pp. 815–859). San Diego: Academic Press.

Lindquist, T. (1995). *Seeing the whole through social studies.* Portsmouth, NH: Heinemann.

Manning, M., Manning, G., & Long, R. (1994). *Theme immersion: Inquiry-based curriculum in elementary and middle schools.* Portsmouth, NH: Heinemann.

Oldfather, P., & Dahl, K. (1994). Toward a social constructivist reconceptualization of intrinsic motivation for literacy learning. *Journal of Reading Behavior, 26*(2), 139–158.

Pradl, G. M. (1996). Reading and democracy: The enduring influence of Louise Rosenblatt. *The New Advocate, 9*(1), 9–22.

Shannon, P. (1993). Developing democratic voices. *The Reading Teacher, 47*(2), 86–94.

Short, K. G., Schroeder, J., Laird, J., Kauffman, G., Ferguson, M. J., & Crawford, K. M. (1996). *Learning together through inquiry.* York, ME: Stenhouse.

Steffey, S., & Hood, W. J. (1994). *If this is social studies, why isn't it boring?* York, ME: Stenhouse.

Weaver, C. (1994). *Reading process and practice: From socio-psycholinguistics to whole language.* Portsmouth, NH: Heinemann.

PART II

Schools as Contributors to a More Equitable and Just Society

CHAPTER 5

Silencing the Lambs

Karen Hankins

> Childhood is something in which we continue to be implicated
> and which is never left behind . . . it persists as something which
> we endlessly rework in our attempt to build an image of our own
> history.
>
> —Jacqueline Rose, *The Case of Peter Pan*

PICTURE THE 1950s IN THE NORTHERN part of the Piedmont just at the base of the mountains. Smell peach orchards, a little factory smoke, and you'll find the South Carolina hamlet I grew up in. On Sundays in starched dresses and shiny shoes we all went to a steepled two-story edifice that smelled of floor wax and a clean mustiness that comes from being closed most of the time. We took our dimes in our hands and our memory verses in our heads and sat in the white primary chairs and sang for Jesus to come into our hearts. The Sunday school teachers were also our schoolteachers.

On Monday morning in less starched, sturdier dresses and scuffed shoes we walked into our schoolrooms and as often as not began the day with a prayer and a scripture. Mrs. Gunter gave candy to those who had been to Sunday school (we wouldn't have dreamed of lying about it), and another teacher gave extra recess if you had your Sunday school paper filled out. You didn't miss school and you didn't miss church. In school I memorized scripture right alongside Robert Louis Stevenson's poetry.

Somehow the romanticized legendary recounting of those days juxtaposes "we could pray/we could read" as one thought, a cause–effect statement. The conservative right gives education in that time an A+, in opposition to the failing grade media gives education today. I lived the legend and proclaim uncategorically: It is a myth.

The blonde-haired, blue-eyed daughter of respected parents, I learned to read before I went to school, and I was clean. Except for talking too much, a complaint that follows me to this day, I was up to standard. But in those A+ days of schooling I never saw a Black child, never met a Jew, had heard of Catholics but never met one. I knew only one person from outside the United States. She was from Germany and "looked normal," but she "talked funny."

Yes, I lived in those days before "edu-fads like whole language and child centered curriculum" (Robinson, 1997) when we could *all* read, according to some. Could we all read the dialogue of the perfect White family who talked in clipped, repeated phrases like, "Oh, oh" and "See Sally?" I suppose it's true that all—well, most—who came to my school could read. Those who couldn't stayed home, like Big Hazel, who only showed up on the first two or three days of school each year. In 2nd grade she sat close to me.

She was 13 and had "never made pass" (never gotten out of 2nd grade). She sat hunched over some scrawling smudged writing, her knees like two mountains flanking the valley of that desk in the too-tight space at the back of the room. She smelled of something I could not identify, but it was unpleasant. I think of her smell, her countenance, the ill-fitting sweater she clutched around her hunched shoulders. She used words like "ain't" and "ova thar" and "hit don't matter none." The teacher frowned at her but didn't call on her again after she said, "Nome [no, ma'am], I reckon I don't want to read." No one asked her, or me for that matter, if we liked the stories we read. No one asked us an opinion or ever gave us a blank piece of paper to fill as we wanted to. There were only right answers in my A+ school of the remembered 1950s, and the teacher had them.

It is difficult to be a product of that education system and yield control of the answers. It is also difficult to hold the memory of Big Hazel and not feel a certain smugness that 13-year-old nonreaders no longer sit in primary grades until they are humiliated enough to stay at home. And yet Big Hazel does show up today in the faces of our children who can't yet break the reading code or in the mouths of children whose narrative patterns are not middle-class and in those who are not White. They come daily, but teachers do not say about them, as they do about the children of the well-educated and well-to-do who increasingly opt for private schools, "We need to do all we can to keep them."

I went to school when a collective national memory believes we all read easily because we "stuck to the basics." A house painter recently explained the presence of his young son working alongside him. As the little boy handed his dad supplies, the painter told me, "My boy wasn't learning anything at school anyway so I home-school him now, and he has to go to work with me a lot. You know things ain't how they used to be—all this loosey-goosey stuff at school. Back when I was in school we didn't have all these problems. We done our work 'cause we had to, we learned to read 'cause the teacher just *made* you do it 'till you *could* do it."

Something in his statement urged me to recognize and better negotiate the borders between myself and children from non-mainstream families. Something in the silent way his "boy" worked, never meeting my eyes, whispering responses to his father, caused me to recoil. In the middle of the night, I remembered.

Bobby Green was in the 2nd grade with me and Big Hazel. He was a Yellow Bird, the low group. The teacher would pull her chair up to the two Yellow Bird rows. She routinely called on them one at a time to stand and read. I dreaded how long it took them to read the story we had made such quick business of the year before. The Yellow Birds struggled over every "look-say" they saw. I especially remember Bobby. He wore glasses and his clothes were not quite right. He stuttered. He shook as he stood to read. It was impossible to tell if he stumbled over the words because of the stutter or because of the inability to decode them. One memorable day the teacher was determined that he would read his page without faltering. She would stop him and say, "Begin again" every time he faltered. After several "begin agains," the tension in that corner captured all our eyes. In my memory the abuse went on at some length. I will never forget the one moment he looked up to risk locking eyes with her. In a silent plea for mercy, born out of a child's belief that adults know best, he whispered, "I c-c-c-can't."

"You can and you will. Begin again—the class would like to go to recess."

We watched Bobby's glasses fill with tears, further impairing his vision. The picture of his hand going to his face to detour the tears from his mouth makes my stomach churn even today. He tried. Oh, how he tried as he stood under the scrutiny of 33 pairs of silent eyes to manage the unveiling of all of his deficiencies at once. The sobs magnified his stutter, the stress interfering with the skills he did have. I wonder which "can't" he referred to in his one attempt at dialogue with the teacher. I can't read? I can't see? I can't speak? I can't be what you want me to be? I can't do what I want so desperately to do?

When she had finally had enough he sat down and buried his face in the crook of his arm, his other hand holding his glasses slightly above his resting head. They waved, a white flag of defeat. As the rest of the class filed out to recess, I looked back at his silent but sobbing shoulders and felt afraid that the teacher would read my thoughts or, worse, that God already knew them. It never occurred to me that hating that Sunday school/schoolteacher didn't damn me to hell. I guess Bobby learned to read. I don't know. I covered my ears the rest of second grade when she went to the Yellow Birds.

Yes, we were schooled during that "A+ time" when prayers were part of school, when some teachers abused the poor, when everybody who *came* to school could read. I went to school during a "stronger America," according to some. Yet it was a fragmented America of Cold War, McCarthyism, and separate but unequal. A friend of mine remembers, "We just didn't have all these problems, you know, we were just all alike then." My own memory of our all-White classroom reveals children marginalized by class, poverty, and isolation. Our lives, appearing so homogeneous from the distance of history, were really worlds apart.

Of course, there *was* the bond of shared silences. Our first three years of school were marked by silence, no-talking rules all day long tangibly reproducing the metaphorical silence born from the absence of self-expression. Big Hazel, Bobby Green, the nameless German girl, and me, Karen Hale, all White, all silenced in school, and all deprived of the collective world-building that could have happened there. What stories did Hazel have to share that were left unheard? What questions were left unasked of Bobby that might have celebrated his own experiences?

Bobby and Big Hazel stare at me from the faces of the children I worry about at school. Today we call them "at risk" and place them in programs called Title I or Special Instructional Assistance. The words we use shape our opinions and our expectations of the children we talk about. It is not the programs but our attitudes toward those served that silence and marginalize and deprivilege. We become a factor in making students "at risk" when we leave off their names in preference of descriptors: Title kids, at-risk kids, the low kids, "those kinds of kids."

So it is that the Big Hazels and Bobby Greens become, year after year after year, exactly what we expect them to become.

"THOSE KINDS OF CHILDREN" TODAY

A teacher's lunch break (aside from being an oxymoron) is brief and the conversation among us is likely to be clipped and to reveal multiple layers of frustration. Often, the lunchtime conversations contribute as much to my dyspepsia as the food does.

Typical lunch-teacher-talk centers around children who are a challenge. With red faces, clenched teeth, stressed shoulders, we lean over our compartmentalized trays of food in an effort to hear over the din of noise. Our complaints fall out at the same rate as the food goes in.

> FIRST TEACHER: How many at-risk children do you have?
> SECOND TEACHER: Out of 26 children I have 12! Now, what am I supposed to do in there? How can I teach?
> FIRST TEACHER: Well, I've got 13. Thirteen children who *can't do anything*! I'm worried about the ones who *can* learn. What am I supposed to do with them?
> SECOND TEACHER: I just want to know what is happening to our school? Where are *these* kinds of children coming from?
> FIRST TEACHER: It gets worse every year!! I mean . . . I love them to death but they are like [giggle] a bunch of monkeys!
> SECOND TEACHER: They can't sit still.
> FIRST TEACHER: They can't keep their mouths shut, can't follow directions! I feel like I'm losing my mind!
> THIRD TEACHER: I was trying to have a lesson and the three or four who "get it" are just waiting patiently while the *low* ones roll in the floor clueless. I mean, I try to involve everybody but you ask a question and they just can't come up with anything! It's like they have no language.
> SECOND TEACHER: Except fussing and cussing!
> FIRST TEACHER: Well, nobody at home ever talks to them!
> THIRD TEACHER: I swear some don't know a pig from a goat. How can we expect them to learn to read?
> FIRST TEACHER: It's all in the home. I say if their parents don't care we cannot be expected to work a miracle at school.

I sit in the frustrating silence of one who cannot contribute or listen to negative conversations about children. I cringe from the degrading language and the measures of marginalization evident in those descriptions. Once, though, I was guilty of similar language and the same rationalizations about differences I observed in children.

Shirley Brice Heath's *Ways with Words* (1983/1996) had much to do with reversing my responses to students. The book is an ethnography that carefully, nonjudgmentally discusses the deep cultural differences in discourse patterns of three distinctly different communities: an all-White mill village, an all-Black working community, and the middle-class towns-people of both races. Recognizing the description of my own White middle-class ways, and the authentic patterns of my parents' childhood mill village ways, validated her descriptions for me. The all-Black community of Trackton came alive. Heath's respectful descriptions of the language development of Trackton's children gave me new eyes for observing the children of similar neighborhoods in my school community. I learned to identify different styles of story and different ways of questioning children, and to understand some ways those differences yield communication difficulties between home and school. I saw how my limited ability to cross cultures keeps me from understanding half of the children I teach. I understood more about the "ways with words" my own parents shed as they began to cross into a middle-class world as young adults. They remembered city attitudes toward mill children. They felt what it was like to be a "that kind of kid." I determined to rid myself of words that oppressed children.

Sarah Michaels' (1981) study of teachers who unknowingly deprivileged African American children's sharing time contributions because their stories were not shaped in a way European American teachers understood forced me to look at the ways in which different cultures tell stories. I determined that I would not privilege one culture over another and that I would listen carefully for the ideas children tried to convey even when I was not smart enough to understand them right away.

James Britton (1993) taught me that talking is the way we shape our understanding of the world and that talk is a direct precursor of successful readers and writers. I determined therefore that my classroom would not be a silent one.

Based on these and other readings, I felt confident that I had placed myself securely on the side of the child. I hoped I would never again have to accuse myself of failing a child based on my unexamined middle-class values. I was proud that I didn't use those lunch-room-teacher-lounge phrases that privilege one kind of family structure over another, or one level of reading over another, or one set of listening behavior over another. It was easy to see *their* faults.

Sometimes, however, I need the stuff of life to come crushing around me in order to realize that I still dwell in a proverbial glass house and should know better than to throw stones. It was painful work to recognize and rid my vocabulary of the subtle but pejorative language of teachers' lounges in favor of a more inclusive one. It took moving away from the classroom for two years and immersing myself in study that centered specifically on issues of power. Now I'm back in the daily rush of school, constantly swimming upstream and usually tired. Living with my students reflectively has at times been difficult.

I want to share an experience with you that places me clearly in the guilty column of the oppressors. Ironically, it takes us back to that metaphorical silence, this time in a classroom of talk. I discovered that some of the participating voices were essentially silenced because they lacked the ingredient of a true listener—me. Simply making talk is not the stuff of communication. In this case, the louder the noise, the more remarkable the silence.

THE SILENCE OF NOT BEING HEARD

I had a special book to share with the children during an especially rainy, stormy spring. The children were five African American second graders, who preferred the descriptor "Black." They had been identified as weak readers and behavior problems, and it seemed at times that they did all they could to live up to their labels. *Storm in the Night* (Stoltz, 1988) was about a grandfather and his young grandson riding out a power outage during a storm. The grandfather reminisced with his grandson about the fear he had of storms as a boy. The point: he faced his fear when his dog, who had been left outside in the storm, needed him.

As I read, the children talked to the book and to each other, a behavior I find completely distracting on one level and full of new information on another. Their overlapping narratives and comments centered around the ways that they would treat the grandson or the dog or the grandfather if they were in the same situation.

What follows is a modified transcription of a tape recording. I took out "uhs," some "ands," and repeated words for ease of reading. The speaker Ivey is a girl; Diounte and Terrence are both boys. Two other boys in the group did not contribute to the conversation.

> IVEY: Well he ought to just smack him!
> TERRENCE: Stupid dog why he let him out the house? If I had me a dog, it be a pit bull and everybody be scared of *him* 'stead of some storm.
> IVEY: You better bring that boy off the porch! He so foolish. Well, sit out there if you want to!
> DIOUNTE: That a white man?

TERRENCE: There this White man live down the corner from my
   grandmama house and he just racist.
DIOUNTE: He live there?
IVEY: See!!! Somebody coming up on your porch an all!
TERRENCE: And he said we was shootin' him a bird and what we
   was doing was saying like, "hey man" to my cousin. [Ges-
   tures a wave] Put his ol' dogs after us. Man I ran!
DIOUNTE: I don't want no dog like that.
IVEY: When the lights go out anyway?
DIOUNTE: Scrawny, can't bite nobody.
IVEY: He might can.
DIOUNTE: Shut up, girl, what you know?
IVEY: *Git dat wet dog out dis house!*
DIOUNTE: Why you didn't keep him inside where he belong den!
IVEY: I'm sayin'!
DIOUNTE: Now *he* comin', bringin' that dog home.
IVEY: Ain't got time to chase your dog boy!
TERRENCE: Did I ask you to bring dis dog back? Your ol' biggity
   self . . .

I stopped reading and looked at them until they were silent. I asked,
"Why does everything I read turn into a story about fighting?" I asked it
as unemotionally as I could; I really wanted to know. But my exasperation
wasn't far below the surface of my face.

In unison the three responded, "Because we live in a bad neighborhood."

I was shocked. For a minute I was speechless.

I cannot verify their meanings, but I believe that their adeptness at
reading small nuances in the faces of adults (like the children of Trackton)
probably signaled my displeasure. Perhaps they answered me as they
were learning to do in school, by assuming that my question had a "known
answer" (Heath, 1996; Michaels, 1983). My displeasure may have signaled
a negative attitude toward them on my part. How many times have they
heard "bad neighborhood" applied to them and who does it come from?
I cannot imagine a teacher telling a child, "You live in a bad neighborhood," in just so many words. Maybe the message has an overtone I
missed. The message may have been embedded in the injunctions that
circulate the neighborhood. It could come from admonitions to stay safe.

So, I read a story where an elderly African American man and his
young grandson sit outside on a porch in the dark. My children live in
a place where they are told to stay inside even in the daytime. If you live
in a place where your mother tells you to stay inside the house, and

where children and the elderly are the easiest prey for violence, the story takes on a completely different face. When the children saw the illustrations in the book, they used the skills they had been taught—to check around themselves at all times, to be smart and not put themselves in danger. They used their knowledge of dogs in their own neighborhood—watchdogs, guard dogs, extra-mouth-to-feed dogs.

My assumption had been that they were unengaged with the text. I didn't really listen to the narratives until I transcribed the tape. I was too busy managing poor behavior. I was too busy reading the text *I* was creating instead of listening to the text *they* collaboratively wrote. As Heath documented with the group-shared reading habits of the neighborhood in Trackton, creating meaning together is not poor behavior; it's just a behavior I don't yet know how to understand, connect with, teach from.

Yet that day the children were doing so many things right. They were bringing necessary knowledge of the world to bear on the story. They were making life-to-text connections (Cochran-Smith, 1984) that I didn't understand. Ivey's narrative exhibited the fussing behavior expected of female children in Trackton: "A good fusser will be a good mama." Bruner says, "What a text is all about is not the actual text but the text that the reader has constructed under its sway" (1986, p. 37). They were "all about that story" by the time they finished. They were responding by creating true stories or "talkin' junk" (Heath, 1983). Stories in that tradition do not teach lessons about proper behavior but about individuals who excel by outwitting rules of conventional behavior. The children's narratives were approximating story precisely that way.

I realize the great liberty I have taken in positioning my children as though they were inside a 1970s community in the Piedmont entering the tide of integration. Even Shirley Brice Heath (1996) points to the differences 20 years have made in communication and interaction patterns in Trackton. "Realignments of time and space, shifts of intimacy and social structures, and new sources of entertainment and consumerism" have influenced the community of Trackton (p. 376). I can only argue that Heath's ethnography says as much about isolated, poverty-ridden African American communities today as Britton's narratives of his own child describe middle-class White children today. These studies give us rich understanding, but we still have much to learn.

Ivey, Diounte, and Terrence used language to organize a representation of their world. They used it to make sense of, predict, and interpret their lives. I did not understand at the time their response to the story. It took several other conversations, several rereadings of my own journal of the event, transcribing the tape, and *time* to sort it out.

The topic-associative dialogue (Michaels, 1983) was related to the book's theme of fear, and to remembering a puppy and a neighbor who addressed a child in a gruff, rude manner. In the end the book was rejected by Diounte: "Boring, think he White."

At least that's what I thought at first. Perhaps he was responding to my inability to follow the discussion. Maybe he meant that *I* thought the character was White and that he was bored with it. The shock passed and I asked them, "What do you mean, you live in a bad neighborhood?"

TERRENCE: Man, people get killed over there.

IVEY: They fight too much.

DIOUNTE: People go after each other with hammers. My daddy went after my mamma with a hammer 'til she got a butcher knife to him.

IVEY: You can't leave nothing outside. You do you might well be sayin' I don't want it no more! 'Cause it ain't gon' be there when you go back out.

TERRENCE: This man beat up this woman so bad he killed her and went into the woods and was hiding in a car back there. And it was lightening and all and the police was checking and stuff.

DIOUNTE: Yeah, well I got a dog that I keep in a pen. He way back in there and I went down there and I seen that car and my dog too. I hide in there spyin' I told somebody. That's where they found him. That man. ["Talking junk," Heath]

IVEY: Go on you ain't

DIOUNTE: What you talkin' girl you just stayin' on your porch cause you scared o' yo' mama!

IVEY: You better be scared yo' ugly mama too, boy!

Knowing where "mama" usually leads us, I scurry to divert the dialogue: "Why do you live there if it's a bad neighborhood?"

IVEY: It all we can afford.

DIOUNTE: My mama can't pay no more.

TERRENCE: But listen . . . here! We savin'

DIOUNTE: Work two jobs don't pay nothin'

TERRENCE: up to get us a real house and when we do! Man . . . and when we do . . . um! I'ma be-e-e—I *mean it!*—I'ma be real, *real* good for like two years. Then I'ma ask my Mama, say, "Mama can I have a basketball goal?" No, no wait forget that . . . no forget that. First I'ma ask for me a puppy that can go in the house with you, and go in your room and be your friend

an all. We gon' do it together. We gon' save all our money
and I'ma help too.

The children and I listened without interruption to Terrence's narrative. Once or twice I heard an affirmative "uh-huh," but for the most part
they shared in silence the place he had created. I heard in that silence
that the hopes and dreams of getting out are the most important future
planning they do. I learned that messages about safety of person and
property are where their parents have put them—right in the front of
their thinking. I heard the universal beacon of saving and working together toward a dream.

I do believe, with James Britton, that oral language precedes and
accompanies reading and writing. I do know that I must understand the
experiences that shape the child who is coming to reading. Understanding
that children share those experiences with me through their talk will help
me to build bridges from the spoken word to the written word. Still, that
day I missed it. Just as surely as my 2nd grade teacher missed what Bobby
and Big Hazel brought to school, just as surely as the teachers at the lunch
table miss what "that-kind-of-kid" brings to "our" school, I missed what
Ivey, Diounte, and Terrence brought to *Storm in the Night*. How many
misses does it take to strike out, to fail a child?

> We cannot afford to ignore all that has gone on before. So often in the past
> we have tried to make a fresh start, at the risk of *cutting off the roots* which
> alone can sustain the growth we look for. (Britton, 1993, p. 129)

REFERENCES

Britton, J. (1993). *Language and learning (2nd ed.).* Portsmouth, NH: Heinemann.
Bruner, J. (1986). *Actual minds, possible worlds.* Cambridge, MA: Harvard University Press.
Cochran-Smith, M. (1984). *The making of a reader.* Norwood, NJ: Ablex.
Heath, S. (1996). *Ways with words.* New York: Cambridge University Press.
Michaels, S. (1981). Sharing time: Children's narrative styles and differential access to literacy. *Language in Society, 10*(3), 423–42.
Michaels, S. (1983). Listening and responding: Hearing the logic in children's classroom narratives. *Theory into Practice, 33*(3), 218–224.
Robinson, M. (1997, October). Crisis in our schools: Education reform. *Investor's Business Daily.*
Rose, J. (1984). *The case of Peter Pan, or the impossibility of children's fiction.* London: Macmillan.
Stoltz, M. (1988). *Storm in the night.* New York: Harper and Row.

CHAPTER 6

Studying Privilege in a Middle School Gifted Class

Mollie Blackburn

I AM A TEACHER OF the language arts and a learner of my students' cultures. From my birth until my college graduation I was immersed in a community composed of people much like myself in terms of race (European American) and socioeconomic status (middle-class). Although this was comfortable for me, it failed to introduce me to the diversity of cultures in my country and my world. So I became a teacher not only to teach, but also to learn.

I began this learning during my first semester at the University of Richmond when I observed an urban elementary classroom. During my program I assisted a teacher in Alternatives to Violence classes, volunteered in a battered women's shelter in Washington, D.C., and eventually student-taught in an urban high school English department. I felt good about teaching because I believed I could have a positive impact on students by helping them to become more effective communicators. I also felt good about learning from my students about their cultures. It seemed like a fair exchange, although I felt a bit of guilt because it seemed I was learning more than they were, particularly during my first year of teaching. But I knew that learning through teaching was what I wanted to do. I considered applying to the Peace Corps, but decided on Teach for America because it offered me the opportunity to serve my country peacefully and develop a more thorough understanding of the cultures that comprise it.

I moved out of my comfortable suburbs of Richmond, Virginia, to teach first in Compton, then in Lynwood, and finally in Boyle Heights, all communities primarily of African American and Latina/o families in Los Angeles. If learning about American cultures other than my own was what I wanted to do, this was a good place to do it. This move demanded that I fully recognize my students as my teachers. This became most obvious to me when my school district failed to close on the day following the announcement of the acquittal of the police officers who beat Rodney King. I drove into Lynwood past much of the destruction that had occurred the previous night. People stared at me with hatred; I represented White people that morning. Smoke billowed from a huge fire visible from my trailer classroom. I felt sad, scared, angry, and resentful. I had a lot to learn. Only a dozen or so students came to school, which closed by noon. But those of us who were there needed to talk, to make sense of our world. We talked about the community's reaction to the verdict and the hatred in people's eyes. I knew I had to be a student, and looked to my students as teachers because they were the people I knew best in the community in which I spent most of my time.

My reliance on students as teachers of their cultures, communities, and themselves continued in my next teaching position in Athens, Georgia. I particularly needed some guidance my second year, when I was assigned to teach Advanced Language Arts, a significant portion of the middle school gifted program. I did not need guidance because the students were so culturally different from me. In fact, they were more like me than any students I had ever taught; most were White, middle-class students who had learned how to succeed in the school system. Instead, I needed guidance in dealing with my conflicting emotions regarding my educational philosophies and my teaching assignment. I sought advice elsewhere from the LEADS group, which Suzanne McCotter had invited me to join. As I introduced myself to the group, I said that I would continue teaching in the middle school but that I'd be teaching Advanced Language Arts.

"You will do *what*?!" Nobody said these words, but I could read them on their faces. Struggling with my feelings, I tried to explain that I like to teach kids, and advanced kids are still kids. I expressed my support for heterogeneous classes and my concerns about the racial and socioeconomic homogeneity in advanced classes. With me, the group questioned the elitism and social power that gifted programs support. Group members alluded to Edelsky's (1994) statement that "The last thing we need, therefore, in creating education for bringing about democracy is to do something that further entrenches some system of domination" (p. 253). As the Advanced Language Arts teacher, it would be too easy to further entrench the system of domination inherent in achievement-grouped classes. I knew that I wanted to struggle, to fight in order to prevent that from happening. Our discussion led toward ways of approaching the assignment with a critical stance. JoBeth Allen suggested that students investigate issues of school organization, such as gifted and remedial classes. Suzanne suggested that I "subvert the system from within." We considered Edelsky's (1994) challenge to become critical "by taking what is seen as business as usual and examining it, figuring out where it came from, what it's connected to, whose interest it serves." I was particularly interested in her specific suggestion to move beyond personal response to literature, to help students take a "sustained look at the societal issues" that are integral to much of the excellent adolescent literature.

AN INQUIRY INTO PRIVILEGE

With these questions, suggestions, readings, and discussions in mind, I met my students—my teachers—and began to develop a plan.

The School

Clarke Middle School includes approximately 650 6th, 7th, and 8th graders. The socioeconomic status of the students varies dramatically. There are few children of old Southern money; generally these children attend the private schools. There are many children of professors from the University of Georgia, and many children of parents who receive support such as public housing and Aid to Dependent Children. There are some children of homeless parents. And, of course, there are many children in between.

In discussing the races of the student body, I struggle with whether to say African American and European American or Black and White. I am more comfortable with the former, focusing on students' ethnicity, than I am with the latter, focusing on the students' colors. However, that year, all of my Black students were African American, but not all of my White students were European American. So I will use Black and White, the words my students used to describe themselves and others. Approximately 53% of the student body was Black, and 46% was White, with 1% from a variety of ethnicities.

The school had self-contained classes designed for students who were mildly, moderately, and severely intellectually disabled. Classes designed for students identified as having learning disabilities and behavior disorders were based on a pullout model. There were language arts and math classes for high-achieving students, and social studies and science classes where teachers could, theoretically, differentiate to meet the needs of their students who were identified as intellectually gifted. The program for these students was based on a facilitation model, in which certified gifted teachers worked in the regular classroom to differentiate instruction for gifted students. As a result, both the teachers certified to teach gifted students and the majority of classroom teachers were assigned to meet the needs of identified gifted students. I worked both as a gifted classroom teacher and a facilitator.

The Kids

I taught 40 students between my two double-block Advanced Language Arts classes. Although their socioeconomic statuses ranged from lower-middle to upper-middle class, there were notably fewer students' families in the lower range. The nine Black students (7 male, 2 female) were on the lower end of the socioeconomic spectrum. So even though the school's student body was 53% Black, less than 23% of my students were Black. Even this embarrassing percentage was better than that of the school as a whole: the percentage of Blacks in Advanced Language Arts classes in my school was only 19 percent.

Students' placements were based on scores on the reading portion of the Iowa Test of Basic Skills (Hoover, Hieronymous, Frisbie, & Dunbar, various years), writing samples, grades in Language Arts during the previous school year, and teacher recommendations. The test scores were intended to provide information about students' reading levels, but there was nothing to indicate students' reading interest. The writing samples were intended to provide information about students' writing levels. The grades were intended to provide information about students' motivation and achievement. The recommendations were intended to provide insight that only experience can offer. Of my 40 students, 64% of them were identified as gifted by the state of Georgia in either of two ways. They either scored in the 99th percentile on a mental ability test, or they scored in the 96th percentile on a mental ability test and scored in the 85th percentile composite or 90th percentile total reading, including reading comprehension or total math. From my perspective, more of my students seemed advantaged rather than gifted. I do not mean to say they lacked gifts, because they did not. However, I saw more evidence of their exposure to that which fosters academic success than that spark of brilliance. They had learned to be good students.

Swirling Thoughts

I kept thinking about the LEADS discussion group, the school, and the kids. I contemplated what we discussed in our LEADS meeting, that we committed ourselves to "teaching in classrooms that educated FOR democracy, for bringing about an end to systemic privilege and domination" (Edelsky, 1994, p. 257). I scrutinized what I saw in the school and what I saw in my classes, that my students and I were not only products of systems of domination, but that we could too easily be perpetuators of these systems. I knew I didn't want that for us, not for them or me, but there we were in our Advanced Language Arts class, immersed in the system, benefiting from our privilege.

I tried to identify why I felt uncomfortable with our class. Theoretically we were only one component in a system that catered to the needs of various learning levels. That's good, right? Of course, our class was the one that catered to the higher learning levels. That was reasonable, wasn't it? In that system, someone had to teach the higher levels, right? Our class did not support elitism any more than any other class, did it? Then why was it that our class looked and felt so different from its complementary components? Why was it so affluent? Why was it so homogeneous? Why was it disproportionally White? What made it elitist? Why didn't it feel right to me?

I did not believe that rich people were innately smarter. I did not believe that White people were innately smarter. I accepted that various literacy levels and multiple intelligences existed, but I did not believe they were defined by socioeconomic status or race. Certainly socioeconomic status could influence academic exposure and foster or hinder abilities, but it could not define learning levels or intelligences. And I celebrated that people had different gifts, some in the realm of language arts and many that were not. But, again, I did not believe that those gifts existed in people according to their socioeconomic status or their race. Certainly socioeconomic status could allow for nurturing of some gifts, but it could not determine their absence or presence. But what did that have to do with our class, and with class in general?

In attempting to calm this mental turmoil and begin to answer my troubling questions, I returned to a way of learning that I had come to value when I learned about the cultures of my students in Los Angeles. I watched and listened to what they knew and learned from their experiences. Although these gifted students were culturally more like me than any other group of students I had ever taught, I still had a great deal to learn from them. Rather than learning about a culture other than my own, we learned about our own culture. We considered what role our culture played in the shaping of other cultures. Together we examined our own privilege.

Developing Plans

The vehicle I chose was literature. We read the young adult novel *Queenie Peavy* by Georgia author Robert Burch (1966). The protagonist, Queenie, is bright, creative, and motivated, like most of my students. However, she is poor, very poor. Her mom works all of the time, and her dad is in jail. Few if any of my students shared the characteristics of Queenie's socioeconomic status and family life. Further, Queenie is not a driven, high-achieving student. She works well when she can focus, but students who tease her about her father and poverty often distract her. My students shared with Queenie academic characteristics but not behavioral characteristics.

I contemplated what Queenie's role could be in our inquiry. I asked my students, my teachers, "Would Queenie be 'right' in our class? Why? Why not? What role would her poverty play? Should it play such a role? Why? Why not?" We could look at "why our class is so White" through the lens of affluence because in Athens the relationship between White people and affluence is a strong one, as is the relationship between Black people and poverty. Certainly these correlations existed throughout our country, and they were heightened in Athens because historically it has been segregated. Now that segregation in public institutions is illegal, many affluent families attend private schools. White people comprised 71% of the county, 85% of the private school population, and 40% of the public school population; Black people comprised 26% of the county, 10% of the population at the private schools, and 54% of the population at the public schools. As we acknowledged the connections between race and socioeconomic status, we looked at Queenie. We examined democratic issues in our community through literature.

Issues of Social Justice in Literature

We read the first third of the novel and met in small discussion groups. I asked students to consider the following question: If Queenie attended our school, would she be in our Advanced Language Arts class? Students discussed and debated the question. I asked that they support their arguments with evidence from the book. We simply generated ideas at this point; we did not come to any conclusions. We read the second portion of the novel and again met in discussion groups. This time, the students brought questions to the groups, including, "If Queenie were in our class,

Table 6.1. Perceived Student Characteristics in the Advanced Language Arts Class—Small-Group Analysis of Fictional Character

Queenie Exhibits	Queenie Fails to Exhibit
Knowledge and skills	Supportive family
Creativity	Positive attitude
Will to work	Attentiveness
Achievement	Good behavior
Perseverance	Respect for self and others
Intelligence	Financial stability
Motivation	Self-control and discipline
	Self-esteem and confidence

how would our class be different?" "Would you want her in here?" "Would you be her friend?" They brought the discussion to life by considering the Queenies in their world. The debate centered around fairness and whether gifted placement should be determined by intelligence or behavior. They seemed to want her in our class, but they wanted her to exhibit what they had learned was appropriate classroom behavior.

After reading the final third of the novel, we returned to the issue of Queenie being "right" for our class, and this brought us to our concluding essay topic, "If Queenie Peavy were a sixth grader at our middle school, would she be in our Advanced Language Arts class?" We developed a format that included 1) what it takes to be placed in our class, 2) what characteristics Queenie exhibited that would get her in, and 3) what characteristics might keep her out. We discussed these questions together, but we decided to come to our conclusions independently. We brainstormed characteristics it takes to be in advanced-level classes. We categorized these characteristics into those Queenie exhibits and those she does not (see Table 6.1). We found evidence in the novel to support each of our claims.

At this point in the inquiry I realized what good teachers my students were. Eight of the 17 traits they identified as indicative of giftedness have been identified by researchers in the field as well. Those traits are knowledge and skills (Baldwin, 1987; Frasier, personal communication, 1996), creativity (Baldwin, 1987; Frasier, personal communication, 1996; Gowan, 1968), perseverance (Renzulli, 1978), intelligence (Baldwin, 1987), motivation (Frasier, personal communication, 1996), attentiveness (Hilliard, 1976; Takas, 1986), and confidence (Gowan, 1968; Hilliard, 1976). Four of the 17 characteristics that my students listed are what the state of Georgia adopted as their regulations a month after our work; they are creativity, achievement, intelligence, and motivation. According to the new regulations, students must exhibit three of these four characteristics in order to be identified as gifted. One exhibition must be a standardized test, and the other two may be grades, products or performances, or motivational scales.

Although Queenie did not have the opportunity to exhibit these characteristics in these ways, my students found evidence to support their claims that she exhibited all four of the characteristics in her own way. For example, Justin found evidence of Queenie's creativity in a scene from the book in which Queenie creates a trap for her nemesis, Cravey Mason. She drags a decaying log over a ravine and tricks Cravey into walking across it. Of course the log breaks and Cravey falls into the ravine. Thus Queenie gets revenge in what Justin and others saw as a creative way. Perhaps the state, as it struggles with learning to identify intellectually gifted students, should also look to students as teachers.

After my students brainstormed necessary characteristics to be placed in our Advanced Language Arts class and found evidence to support whether or not Queenie exhibited them, I conducted mini-lessons on outlining, persuasive essays, and a "could/should/would" analysis technique. Then students began to work more independently. Each student made an outline that included the following:

1. The characteristics it takes to be in an advanced class, and why
2. The characteristics Queenie exhibited or lacked, backed by supporting evidence, and
3. Their conclusion as to whether Queenie would be "right" for our class, based on evidence from the book and our class investigation

Finding Depth

Although our discussions and products showed sincere thought, they lacked depth when addressing the issue of socioeconomic status. In an effort to politicize our brainstorming session, I added "family support" and "socioieconomic status/income level" to our list of characteristics. Some students did not comprehend my suggestion and attempted to address the issues anyway, perhaps out of obligation. The results were messy; for example, Joe wrote, "You have to behave good or be disciplined and be wealthy or have socioeconomic status." Several students mentioned that one needs to "have" socioeconomic status to be in advanced classes. We had lengthy discussions about their definitions and stereotypes about welfare, but I didn't help the students make the connection to understanding socioeconomic status. If I were doing this again, I would.

Our discussion of welfare was prompted when Queenie's best friend's family began receiving public assistance. The family was reluctant to accept it, but since the children were suffering from poor nutrition, there was little choice. By observing this family's experience, we created definitions of welfare based on the book. Next we looked at dictionary definitions. Then we interviewed people at home about welfare and shared the information we gathered. Finally we wrote how we, as individuals, defined welfare and what we thought and felt about it. Students seemed to discuss the issue of welfare as fluently as many adults, and more fluently than some politicians.

Six months after our work with Queenie, I interviewed students about the novel. Students could communicate the meaning of welfare much more clearly than the meaning of socioeconomic status. They even recalled the discussion format that we used to get at the meaning of welfare. I would use the same format for understanding socioeconomic status. First I would introduce the concept of socioeconomic status in terms of being rich, middle-class, and poor. I would ask students to interview an adult and learn what the term means to the adult; then we would share the various ideas. Next students would create their own definitions. I would ask them to identify the socioeconomic statuses of various public figures, before and after they became well known. I would facilitate a discussion in which students would hypothesize the impact of those people's socioeconomic statuses on their success. Then I would bring the issue back to Queenie. What socioeconomic status is she? How do you imagine that is evident in her home life? Her school life?

I think a more developed understanding of the concept of socioeconomic status would have encouraged more thoughtful responses to the essay question. Although students struggled with the term, they certainly recognized the concept of cultural capital. Katsillis and Rubinson (1990) wrote, "The cultural capital hypothesis is based on the finding that family background is reflected in differential academic rewards" (pp. 270–271). My students' recognition of this concept became apparent in their responses to the essay question mentioned above.

Some students expressed clearly that Queenie would not and should not be in our class because of her behavior. Even though they acknowledged her intelligence, they emphasized behavior. Bob wrote, "Queenie would not be in our class because it is a reward for people who have good behavior, and she does not have good behavior." He related that he behaved better than those not placed in advanced classes. He seemed to believe that he deserved to be in our class as a reward, rather than as a way of meeting his intellectual needs. Bob and some of his peers seemed to support what I perceived as a flaw in the program, the promotion of elitism.

Many students expressed clearly that Queenie would and should be in our class because of her intelligence. They acknowledged her poor behavior as a hindrance, but they emphasized her abilities. Mary wrote, "Queenie may not always have perfect behavior, but she has brains. She is very intelligent. She is a hard worker. . . . I believe Queenie should be in advanced classes." Tommy thought, "She still should behave, but that shouldn't be what keeps her out of advanced language arts." Miriam offered the most thoughtful explanation when she wrote,

> I believe Queenie should be in advanced classes. She is smart and in need of a challenge. She needs to be around other kids with high intelligent levels like herself. A bad temper like Queenie's should not prevent a person from being in an advanced class, if they are smart. Queenie needs to be in to improve her skills, and have work at her level. Also being in an advanced class would be more interesting than a non-advanced class, and make her bored less of the time, so she would not need to amuse herself by being bad.

Miriam suggests that the school is responsible for challenging and engaging its learners, and in so doing can help students behave well. Mary, Tommy, Miriam, and many of their peers seemed to support what I perceived as a goal for our program, the meeting of intellectual needs based on actual intellect.

It did not surprise me that no one wrote that Queenie would have been placed in advanced classes but should not be there. However, I was impressed by Rufus's thoughtful essay, in which he wrote,

> I believe that Queenie should be in advanced classes, but she wouldn't be, [because of] how kids are put into classes. Queenie would be put in lower classes because kids are put in classes based on behavior, more than intelligence. I think Queenie is very smart, but she can't control her temper. I think it is very unfair how things would turn out.

Rufus clearly combined the reality of the program, that behavior keeps you out, with the ideal of the program, that intelligence gets you in.

My students' responses to Queenie, one another, and the essay question taught me that they are not only good students, but also good people who wanted to be part of a program that they could believe in and be proud of. As their teacher, I wanted to help them distinguish the ideal, what they wanted to see in their program, and the real, what actually existed. Perhaps recognition of this distinction could begin to balance the elitism fostered by their advanced placement.

LITERACY EDUCATION FOR A DEMOCRATIC SOCIETY

So we began to find answers to the questions I overtly asked myself and covertly asked my students. By giving Queenie more thought, extracting her from the novel, and inserting her into our lives, we examined why we were in our advanced class and what that actually said about us. Did it say that we were smarter than others, and therefore in many eyes "better" than others? Or did it say that we had advantages, including edges of confidence, that many people lack? We acknowledged and learned about our social power; we struggled with the impact it had on the Queenies of our community. I cannot say we answered the questions that arose, and are listed here, but we certainly grappled with the issues. Serving yet again as my teachers, my students guided me in exploring these questions from their perspectives:

- *Why was our class so relatively affluent?* When affluence nurtured the skills, attitudes, and behaviors that determined students' placement in advanced classes, those placed were those who were affluent. And that did not feel right.
- *Why was it so homogeneous? Why was it so White?* When affluence and race are so tightly bound, as they are in Athens, the affluent White kids are those placed in the advanced classes, where they learn to feel as if they are in some ways better than others. And that did not feel right.
- *What made our class elitist?* When students believed that they were in advanced classes as a reward because they behaved better than others, they could have easily learned to believe that they were better than others. Linda and Eddie provided evidence of this mentality. Linda wrote, "To be in advanced classes you must have good characteristics." In explaining that Queenie could have been in our class but would not have been, Eddie wrote, "I think Queenie could be a good person if she would have a good attitude." He substituted "be in our class" for "be a good person," implying that only "good people" were in our Advanced Language Arts class. Certainly that did not feel right.
- *Why didn't it feel right?* Affluent White students already had an edge of confidence, perhaps a sense of elitism, that had facilitated their placement in advanced classes. I did not want to foster that edge of confidence

in our placement in advanced class; that did not feel right. It felt better, to me and I believe to my students, to examine the social structures in our own lives and in our classroom, so that we could begin to deal with an issue that is of great importance to adolescents: fairness. It is also the foundation of a democratic society.

CHALLENGING PRIVILEGE

Teachers who have a say in the design of how classes are constituted can and should argue for heterogeneous classes. Those who do not can argue for multiple indicators of ability for "advanced" classes. Teachers whose voices are heard by administrators can resist teaching classes that promote racism and classism, as many "gifted" classes seem to do, based on who is admitted. Those whose voices are heard primarily by their students can examine, with their students, the social structures of their classrooms, schools, and lives.

REFERENCES

Baldwin, A. Y. (1987). I'm black but look at me, I am also gifted. *Gifted Child Quarterly, 31,* 180–185.

Burch, R. (1966). *Queenie Peavy.* New York: Viking Press.

Edelsky, C. (1994). Education for democracy. *Language Arts, 71,* 252–257.

Frasier, M. (May 21, 1996). Personal communication, Athens, GA.

Gowan, J. C. (1968). Issues in the education of disadvantaged gifted students. *Gifted Child Quarterly, 12*(2), 115–119.

Hilliard, A. G. III (1976). *Alternative IQ testing: An approach to the identification of gifted "minority" children* (Report No. 75175). San Francisco, CA: San Francisco State University. (ERIC Document Reproduction Service No. ED 147 009)

Hoover, H., Hieronymous, A., Frisbie, D., & Dunbar, S. (various years). Iowa test of basic skills. Riverside, CA: Riverside.

Katsillis, J., & Rubinson, R. (1990). Cultural capital, student achievement, and educational reproduction: The case of Greece. *American Sociological Review, 55,* 270–279.

Renzulli, J. S. (1978). What makes giftedness?: Re-examining a definition. *Phi Delta Kappan, 60,* 108–184.

Takas, C. A. (1986). *Enjoy your gifted child.* Syracuse, NY: Syracuse University Press.

CHAPTER 7

Walking the Tightrope on Diversity

Eurydice Bouchereau Bauer

WHEN I CAME TO THIS COUNTRY at the age of 10, I spoke French Creole and French, the languages of my native Haiti. I had never heard a person speak English; I had no conception of the United States and of race relations. Once in the United States, I was taught in subtle and not-so-subtle ways that I was a "minority." Although I am a person of color, I had never thought of myself in this way, nor did I know what it really meant. I had to learn about both the African American and the European American culture in the United States. I recognize that my minority status in the United States makes it a little easier for me to learn about the African American culture, but there was more to the ease of my learning than color. Color by itself does not establish membership. I had to be willing to learn and to appreciate what African Americans have to offer.

I spent most of my adult years in the Midwest, where I earned my bachelor and master's degree from the University of Iowa, taught in the Iowa City schools, and earned my doctorate at the University of Illinois. In both Midwestern cities, I was clearly a minority. I faced discrimination in both towns. It was not unusual for me to enter a restaurant or a store and have the waiter or clerk help the European American person behind me before speaking to me. In most instances, I made it clear to the clerk or waiter that I had been overlooked, which was enough to make them turn red and do the appropriate thing.

Currently, I am teaching at the University of Georgia (UGA), which in recent years has made some good-faith efforts to diversify its faculty and students. This is a slow process and the faculty and students remain predominantly European American. In the college of education, a growing number of instructors are committed to going beyond the superficial approach when presenting issues of social justice in their classrooms. However, many others ignore or briefly mention issues such as racism, culturally inappropriate practice, and power relations in their classrooms. The decision on the part of some faculty members to dismiss these issues as central to the educational goal of the college has great consequences, given the fact that our college of education prepares the largest number of teacher candidates in Georgia, which is 30% African American and has a growing Hispanic population.

THE TENSION ON THE ROPE

Although I teach both undergraduate reading methods courses and graduate courses in reading, my focus here will be on my undergraduate students. Typically, I teach two consecutive reading methods courses to the same 27 students. My students are predominantly European Americans and represent a range in socioeconomic background, with the largest group coming from the middle class.

Many of my European American students enter my classroom with life experiences that make it extremely difficult for them to come to terms with the reality that *I* am their instructor for two quarters. Many are accustomed to seeing and interacting with African Americans in service-related roles. As one student put it, "I am not comfortable around you, it's like I am going to say something wrong . . . My only experience with interacting with an African American person on a regular basis is with the lady who works for us." The university context in some respects perpetuates the ways in which people of color are viewed. For example, most of our custodial staff are African Americans. By contrast, most of the professors and students are European Americans. When these students encounter me, a Haitian American, they bring all of their conceptions and misconceptions of "other" to the interaction. In order to adequately discuss with my preservice students how to educate other people's children (Delpit, 1995), I had to acknowledge my students' superficial experiences with people who are different from them. According to Willis (1997), "acknowledgment of the history, attitudes, and sometimes baggage that we bring to class helps move us toward change" (p. 156).

Living and teaching in the South meant that I had to deal with overt racism both in the community and in the classroom. For example, I went to a local store to buy a few things for my daughter. Right in front of me a matronly European American woman used her check and went through the line very quickly. When it was my turn the young lady decided to check my check against the list she kept of bad checks. I was not on that list. She then went to the phone and called for clearance. I became irritated and demanded that she explained what she was doing. She tried to appease me by telling me that this happened to a man earlier who was also upset. I asked her if he was also African American. She stared at me and continued with her activity. I later learned that this is common practice in this store. It was the last time I visited it.

My interaction with my students in the classroom was also different from my teaching experience in the Midwest. For example, when I taught at the University of Illinois, undergraduate students repeatedly challenged what they were asked to do. Although at times I felt that some questioned having a person of my ethnicity teaching them, they only questioned classroom assignments, not my authority. However, when I started teaching my reading courses at UGA some students felt it was appropriate to begin conversations with me by saying things such as "You need to rethink . . . ," or "I don't think you understand . . . ," always stressing the *you* in their statements. It was as if they were the people in charge of the class. Although I disliked the way students interacted with me, I wondered if I was not reading more into their words then necessary. I questioned a European American colleague who taught the same cohort of students about the way they interacted with her. During the course of the conversation, it became quite clear that students were not using the same tone or language in her class as they were using in my class. This lack of respect was emotionally draining.

As I pondered this problem of blatant disrespect, I entertained four options. First, I could quit and take a position someplace else. However, I felt this would be a personal defeat, as though I had somehow let a few students "run me out." Second, I could adopt the ethos that methods courses should simply focus on technical content. I could teach them about rudimentary elements of teaching reading and ignore the social elements. But I was uncomfortable with this hands-off approach because it meant that the children who have repeatedly felt unwelcome in our schools would continue to feel this way. I agree with Diamond and Moore (1995) that "teachers need [to have] additional social and cultural knowledge" in order to meet the needs of their increasingly culturally and linguistically diverse students. Third, I could let the bitterness consume me and go on an angry crusade. In the long term I did not think I could live with the type of person I would become. Lastly, I could try to redirect the tension that I had been experiencing and turn it into something productive. I recognized that the latter would be the hardest to live with in the short run, but if successful, the most rewarding in the long run.

The decision to address the tensions and redirect them in order to "educate," in a broader sense, my students meant merging my personal and professional life. I decided to open up my pain and struggles to my students so that they could see a professor and a mother before them. If they could not see me as a person, I did not think it was likely that they would see children like my daughter as people either. Accepting the challenge to address the tensions in the classroom meant that I was constantly walking a line where I had to create a balance between my need to respond to what I am experiencing as a person of color and the need to create a genuine dialogue that will both preserve my self-dignity and bring the talk to a critical level. Often, I did not feel I had the luxury of simply defending myself when I felt attacked. To do that would mean possibly turning off the dialogue I had hoped to begin. The lines between personal and professional became blurred and teaching therefore became much more challenging. This chapter is in part a description of my students and their reactions and responses to my conscious efforts to draw all of them into a discussion, but it is also about my personal struggle to deal with my emotions as I embarked on this journey.

STEPS TOWARD GENUINE DIALOGUE

There are a number of reasons why I address social and political issues in my classroom and why I hope they will start a genuine dialogue. On a smaller scale, my students repeatedly showed me that they entered my classroom having had no or little experience at the university with people of color. At the beginning of each quarter, I am often given the look of disbelief by a handful of my students as they learn that I will be their instructor for the course. Some students assume before the class starts that I am the teaching assistant instead of the professor. Other faculty members meeting me for the first time have also presumed that I was a student.

A second reason, and a more substantial one, for deciding to address issues of social justice in my teaching of reading is my own personal belief that unless all educators can openly discuss the social context of schooling as a possible reason for school failure in general and reading failure in particular, we are doomed to fail to meet the needs of many more children. My convictions were repeatedly confirmed by student comments such as, "If these parents cared about their kids they would show up for teacher conferences and read to their children at home" when we discussed children who are economically deprived, linguistically diverse, and/or represent various ethnic groups. Students often failed to see their comments as "blaming the victim" despite my efforts to label them as such.

Challenging Assumptions: "It's Their Fault They Are Not Succeeding"

As part of our classroom discussion on teaching reading to English as a Second Language (ESL) students, our class worked in small groups to discuss assigned articles that were designed to provide them with information on what teachers can do to help ESL students. One group's perspective was that immigrant parents should accept part of the blame for their children's failure. They contend that immigrant parents should teach their children English. The members of the group repeatedly stated that they could not be held responsible for students who do not make adequate progress. They argued that the parents knew they were coming to an English-speaking country. As one student said, "It is a doggy dog [sic] world out there and parents have to understand that!" It was a foregone conclusion: These students could not perform well in school given their linguistic limitations.

This discussion troubled me on a number of levels. As an educator, I am always alarmed when in-service or preservice teachers from the onset have given up on some of their students. On a more personal level, I found myself reflecting on my immigrant status and becoming enraged. I had experienced first-hand what can happen to a student's self-esteem when teachers have that attitude. The discussion took me back to sixth grade, Mrs. Hannig (all student and teacher names in this chapter are pseudonyms), and a painful recollection of the sentence diagramming lesson. I had been in the country for two years. My conversational English was good enough to interact with most people, but my academic English skills were less prominent. As I recall, Mrs. Hannig made the distinction quite clear.

> ME: Teacher, I don't get it.
> [Mrs. H repeated what she had said]
> ME: Teacher, I still don't get it
> MRS. H: (very frustrated) That is the problem. If you people don't learn the language, how are you supposed to amount to anything? You will not amount to anything until you learn how the English language works.

In the presence of my classmates I listened to how my family had failed me by bringing me to the United States and most important, how I would not amount to anything. I always wondered if Mrs. Hannig knew that I spent the rest of the day memorizing her phrases so that my tutor could explain them in French. Here I was again, many years later, facing students who seemed to have similar views. Yet I recognized that my students needed to make these statements in order for us to have a genuine discussion on the role of teachers in helping ESL students learn to read. Given my students' need, I decided to tell them another personal story about Sister Alice, who would not let my limited English proficiency interfere with all of the things she had to teach me that year. We discussed Sister Alice's lack of French speaking skills and how her determination to "teach" me led her to employ good teaching strategies that were consistent with second language acquisition. For example, she encouraged me to do my writing assignments in French. During recess and, more often, as homework assignment, I would translate my ideas into English, using a French/English dictionary. Twice a week, she and I met after school and discussed my writing. She was always accepting and supportive of my efforts, and at the same time never lost sight of the next skill I needed to learn. I contrasted that with Mrs. Hannig's view of me and my lack of interest in school that year.

Reflections on Previous Attempts

My first attempts to openly discuss what my students viewed as "controversial issues" were often met with a great deal of resistance. As one of my students stated in her course evaluation, "I was very frustrated in this class, . . . many of the articles were not helpful . . . I wanted to simply learn to 'teach' reading." Some students resisted what I had to say because *I* was the instructor—"I felt very intimidated by the instructor and did not feel comfortable around her." Another stated, "She had a definite agenda . . . I came to this class to learn how to teach reading . . . I know some of her issues are important, but it is more important that I can teach reading." A few of my students found my willingness to share my past experiences with them enlightening. One of my European American students wrote in a personal note to me, "During my time at Georgia, I have *never* [her emphasis] had such a dedicated and intelligent teacher. Thanks for setting a wonderful example of what or who a teacher should be . . . I now know the teacher I want to become." My observations of my students led me to two conclusions that would shape my subsequent interactions with them: (1) Some students in the class were open to talking about education in a broader sense. These students liked the merging of reading content with issues related to the students they will teach. This meant that I would have some allies when certain topics emerged. (2) A majority of the class did not feel comfortable with this "new" way of looking at their learning. They were happy to simply focus on the reading content without looking at the social issues.

I knew these issues would make my students and myself uncomfortable, but in order to successfully participate in conversations that are liberating, I needed to take part in what bell hooks called "engaged pedagogy" (1994). I needed to explore my own personal issues as I assisted students to do the same. I decided to weave in two educational texts on social change, which I selected because the authors used personal narratives to help the reader better understand issues of race in education. During the first quarter, students read *Dreamkeepers* by Gloria Ladson-Billings (1994), responded in their journals, and discussed it in class. The second quarter, students read *White Teacher* by Vivian Paley (1979) and did the same. During the first quarter, they read with an elementary student once a week for 30 minutes. The second quarter, they tutored a struggling reader for 30 minutes every day for 4 weeks. The struggling reader had to be of a different background from the tutor. They wrote about their field experience in light of their readings. I used the tape recordings of our class discussions of both books and students' journal reflections to help guide subsequent interactions with my students.

Although both texts addressed the teaching of African American students, the students approached the books differently. As a group, the class preferred *White Teacher* over *Dreamkeepers*. The students disliked *Dreamkeepers* because they felt it was not written for them. They read the book as a text that was written by an African American woman for African American teachers on what to do with African American students. Despite my attempts to point out the fact that three of the eight excellent teachers were European Americans, they did not see or hear themselves in that dialogue. One student said, "For some reason, this book makes me feel bad, like I am going to be a horrible racist teacher who hurts the minority students." Others agreed. Some of the students were frustrated with the disheartening statistics on the failure rate for African Americans and the demographics of the teaching force. The tension created by these two facts remained throughout the two quarters.

Our second reading, *White Teacher*, presented the issues from a frame of reference that was more comfortable for the students. The students found more of themselves in Paley's reflections. Students repeatedly said, "I have to respect just how honest she is about these issues." Paley gave voice to what some of my students would not normally talk about. For example, one European American student wrote in her journal, "I really like this book *White Teacher*, I guess it's because I can relate to Paley so much, because deep down, I'm uncomfortable with the thought of having to really confront race issues in my classroom." Another student wrote, "I appreciate reading this book and hearing about another person's insecurities and discomfort in working with children and parents of different ethnic background." For many of my students, Paley situated their learning in a historical and social context that helped them understand.

Diversity Matters: Students Helping Students

A novel dimension to this class was its diversity. My cohort in the winter and spring of 1997 was one of the most diverse groups of students ever to go through our college of education. Many classes are exclusively European American women. However, in a class of 27, two of the students were males, two were African American females, one was a Caribbean female, one was a Chinese American female, and one was a Japanese ESL female. Their backgrounds were as interesting as the perspectives that they introduced. The diversity of the class was influential in shaping our discussions.

The students who were comfortable in leading our discussions on diversity developed a sense of solidarity with one another and with me. They regularly visited my office to discuss issues raised in class and to seek individual assistance. Two of my female students, one African American and one European American, continually pushed the others to a level of self-awareness that maintained a sort of healthy tension when discussing the books. Erica, a European American female from the South, brought to our discussion a deep understanding of the larger multicultural issues because of her background in African American Studies. But her insights came with a price. She was often quite frustrated with having to explain to other European Americans her decision and commitment to teach in Metro-Atlanta in predominantly African American populations.

> When I tell people I pursued a certificate in African American Studies, they almost always follow-up with the question "why?", and I can read their minds because of their look of confusion and disbelief. The look seems to cry out " . . . but you are white?"

The other student who challenged us was originally from New York, but had lived in the Atlanta area for a number of years. Cara, an African American female, repeatedly forced us to take a closer look at the readings. From her perspective, good intentions about teaching other people's children were fine, but in the end could not revolutionize education. In a discussion on culturally relevant teaching of reading she explained:

> I feel, before an individual can truly become a culturally respon-sive teacher, he/she needs to first self-examine their own percep-tions concerning cultural groups, ethnic groups, religious groups and so on. One needs to confront their personal biases, and their misconceptions and then work to eliminate such barriers in order to become a culturally responsive teacher. If we fail to do that, it will inhibit the teacher from seeing the value in acknowledging and respecting various cultures and, as a result, will have a detri-mental impact on students' ability to learn.

Cara and Erica helped move us beyond declarations by some students that they were not racist and all teachers should love students. What we often had to struggle with was how we would reach the goal of accepting all students and helping them emotionally and intellectually. Cara and Erica said things that I could not say to the students. They were key in changing the tone of the classroom.

Listening in New Ways

Some of the students were taking a "tourist approach" (Sleeter, 1994) and were not internalizing what they were reading. Their reading was not causing them to think about the way they see the world and therefore the way in which they respond to it. Instead they relied on more socially accepted responses without critically examining them. For example, dur-ing our discussion of *White Teacher* the students criticized Paley for not accepting diversity from the onset. They argued that more could be learned from having a diverse classroom than a homogeneous one. A small group of European American students pointed out that the goal of embracing diversity is much harder to realize, and challenged the class to examine itself.

> SUZY: You know, as we speak about these issues and their relation-ship to literacy, I find it interesting that no one has taken a closer look at the way we interact in this class. Every instruc-tor since we started levels mentioned that we were the most diverse group of students they have ever had here. I think that is pretty sad because we are still predominantly white. I wonder if any of us have stopped and examined the relation-ship between what we say we want in our classroom [a mix

of students], the type of interaction we say we want to have and the lack of interaction we have across ourselves.

CECI: What do you mean?

SUZY: I mean we have other students in this class who typically aren't represented in classes with us, but we do not go beyond simply being polite. I don't know, all of this just started me thinking. I know for myself that most of my friends are white like me. I am just saying it makes you think when we keep saying all we need is the opportunity.

A number of students were starting to see the issue of educating all of our students in a broader sense. They were learning that it is not as easy as learning a few teaching tricks. Yet I knew that many more of my students were not at this point. I spent many sleepless nights pondering my role. The old adage "If you reached one student you have made a difference" did not comfort me. I could not help but wonder about the ones I did not reach and the possibility of them teaching children like my daughter. The more we opened our discussions on diversity, the more I realized what many of my students did not know and the more uncomfortable I became.

The Search for Generalizations

Many of my students were genuinely at a loss as to what they were supposed to do about the political and stratified nature of schooling. Some felt they needed explicit information on what they should and should not do. In particular, they wanted someone like Cara to personalize the problem. They wanted her to speak about her comfort or discomfort about these issues as someone who has been in a minority in many classrooms. Two European American students engaged Cara in a discussion on the impact of race on learning.

ANNETTE: You have been a minority but you have also been . . . look where you are, in college.

BETTY: I think it has to do with socioeconomics. What we are talking about doesn't have a lot to do with race, but with money. Whether kids are Black or White, if their school doesn't have money they are not going to receive the teachers that they should or receive a good education.

CARA: I don't know. Socioeconomic status isn't all of it. I mean, I'm not poor and I am not rich either and yet people have a perception of me that is contextualized by the fact that I am in an all-White classroom or whatever. This perception is there despite the way I speak or present myself. That barrier is still there . . . So, my question would be, how do we get beyond this so that we are better than what I've experienced all my life? I am asking whether or not people can really put their biases aside?

ANNETTE: I think a lot of times people do stuff that is going to offend someone else and you are not even going to know it. I think this is about awareness, coming to terms with what you really feel even if you learn that you didn't mean to be a racist but . . .

BETTY: Personally, I have to learn to not let it hurt my feelings if I inadvertently offended someone. It doesn't make me a bad person because I messed up and said something that hurt somebody.

This need for students to have some "other" explain to them what the situation is really like emerged repeatedly. I often found myself frustrated listening to these discussions. Implicit in these questions was the belief that European Americans could not be expected to know about "others" because they have not been in that situation. My students often failed to see that it is their responsibility to learn about "others" and that it is not the responsibility of the students of color to "teach" them. Perhaps my frustration is related to my Haitian American perspective. I am often perplexed how I, an immigrant with little knowledge of the United States, could make some progress in learning about ethnic groups in this country, while some European Americans are less knowledgeable on these topics. These are the times when I relied on Cara and others to say to the class "your lack of knowledge of 'others' in the United States is a result of choices that you have made." Then I could stress looking for daily opportunities for learning about themselves and others in their community and in their classrooms.

Many of the students were looking for generalizations for why a disproportionate number of minorities were failing in our schools, and a few students were quite confident that they knew why. A turning point occurred in a class discussion of parents, especially poor parents, in the educational process.

SAIRA: This past week in the field, all I saw were parents not showing up for conferences. I know Ladson-Billings and Paley are talking about strong connection between families and the school, but what happens when the parents just don't care about their children? So what are you supposed to do to get your parents involved? Their lack of involvement shows to me that they have other more important things in their lives.

ANNA: Yeah, maybe feeding their children. You know, like work! You have to understand, it is important to have school contact, but it is more important to feed your kid.

SAIRA: Well, it just seems like it was contagious, like one mother called and said "I can't make it" and then ten minutes later another called.

CHRIS: They probably never had anybody that went into their conferences when they were little. It's a cycle.

TEACHING ASSISTANT (an African American doctoral student and single mother): I think we have to keep in mind that some of the parents in town have hourly jobs and have to work late on a regular basis. Some of the people in town work at the plant and they have to do mandatory overtime like twelve hours a day for six days. So when do you want them to conference? Keep in mind that then there is also the issue of sitters and money for the sitter. These are real-life issues that people struggle with every day.

SAIRA: So what is a teacher to do?

EB: First of all you get to know your students, their situation, and then you work with and around it. I think we are going to have to look at parent/teacher interactions that extend beyond seven thirty to three o'clock.

SAEHEE: I guess it could even be phone conversations. In some cases it would help some of the parents that I learned about in the field. One parent has a number of kids and . . .

SAIRA: That is just ridiculous! What I want is parental involvement.

ANNA: What else can we do beyond calling?

TA: One teacher I know who is really dedicated to her students went and met one parent in the plant at seven thirty in the morning and then went to school.

SAIRA: I can't help it that when I am out in the schools and I learn about their home life I can't help but respond differently to them. I don't feel as comfortable and I have bad thoughts. I can't help it. I know it isn't right, but I just can't help it.

Making Learning Personal

This discussion was quite troubling to me. On the one hand, students wanted to know how to reach the kids who are not making it. Yet many did not want to deviate much from what they perceived their role should be. I did not feel I could openly voice my dissatisfaction with the discussion, or say to the student who was experiencing "bad thoughts" that she should find another profession. All I could do was to think about my daughter with such an instructor. Even though the answer to how to better educate our children rests on having candid discussions, this very candor created mixed feelings for me.

I encouraged students to bring their personal stories to our discussions and to relate them to the class readings. Yet some of their stories created a great deal of discomfort for me. Some of these stories were revelations of sorts for my students and for me. Richard wrote that he found the children's discussion in Ladson-Billings's book on the color of Egyptians interesting given his background. He described himself as a "southern, farm-raised, Caucasian male, raised in a biased and discriminating culture," who couldn't help but reflect on the way "the white church has always depicted Jesus as white." He found himself wondering what members of his church would say if anyone tried to depict Jesus as anything other than a European. He recalled hearing as a child "that blacks are from the tribe of Israel that received a curse—their skin color." His later journal and class discussions went on to question the things he learned about "others" as a child and the underlying racism.

Other stories created even stronger discomfort in me. Carol described her grandfather's open racism and hate for everyone who is not White. Her mom and dad were not racist, but it was understood that no one should challenge her grandfather. Carol wrote, "Racism has always been a part of the South and [I] suspect that's not going to change with my granddad." Although she does not challenge her grandfather openly, she challenges him in the way she has chosen to raise her family.

I wondered whether Richard, Carol, and others could overcome years of indoctrination about minorities. I also wondered whether their comments indicated that they were moving beyond the limit of their experiences. After all, they were openly questioning their experiences and reflecting on what it means for their teaching. As a professor, I was encouraged by their level of self-reflection, but I could not help feeling that this should have occurred much earlier in their program. As a parent, I questioned whether some of my students were ready to teach my daughter and other people's children (Delpit, 1995).

LESSONS FOR EDUCATORS

Despite my reactions to our discussions, I knew in my heart that the type of talk taking place was necessary and could lead to learning beyond the domain of reading. I conclude this chapter with what I learned as well as what I believe my students learned.

Critical explorations of social injustice can begin in the classroom. According to literacy researchers (e.g., Barrera, 1992; Delpit, 1988; Reyes, 1992), teacher education courses are ideal for helping students expand their cultural knowledge. The classroom may not be the place where all answers are found, but it may provide the opportunity to systematically explore what we bring to the classroom and its possible impact on students' learning. For example, toward the end of the second quarter, one of my European American students wrote that another student in the class openly shared with her and a few others that she was racist and that her views were separate from her teaching. "I really did not think much about what she said when she said it. Now, I just keep telling myself no one with that sort of conviction will ever meet the needs of your daughter. This saddens me, but I don't know what to do. I almost don't want to be in education with people like that."

Her recognition that someone with racist views could be detrimental to minority students is important. However, more important is her awareness of my daughter, and the many others like her, as unique individuals. In her statement, she recognized my daughter's color, and saw her as a person of worth. Such insight by some of my students provided me with a geat deal of hope.

Educators must do a better job at selecting education majors. Members of the class made differential progress toward understanding the role of teachers in teaching children of color, which is expected given their different entry points to the dialogue on diversity. However, I am disheartened that a student with strong racist convictions can move through our program undetected. One explanation is that many instructors do not explore the issues presented in this chapter beyond a superficial level. A second explanation is that my presence in the classroom makes these issues much more real and concrete. My constant presence may stand to make a difference in the previously impervious views of some of my students. However, if professors, such as myself are to avoid falling victim to burnout, they must have a strong support system that assists them in their teaching.

The classroom dialogue must begin within the social context that is most comfortable for the students. I began with Ladson-Billings's (1994) book, hoping it would provide concrete examples of what successful teachers were doing in their classrooms. I am still convinced that students must have models of good teaching in order to provide them with an appropriate teaching repertoire. However, in the future I will start with Paley (1979), a White teacher, like most of my students, in order to squarely place the students in the center of the dialogue. My goal is to start with stories of their own experiences with people of color, which would legitimate and support my students as "people who matter, who can participate in their learning, and who in doing so can speak with a voice that is rooted in their sense of history and place" (Diamond & Moore, 1995). In addition, sharing their experiences around a narrative line allows them the opportunity to create a link with their pasts and outline a path for their future, while developing a better understanding of the lives of others (Narayan, 1991).

LESSONS FOR STUDENTS

Embracing diversity is hard work. The students who identified with me and my struggles started using their insights to also evaluate their practicum classrooms. They reported feeling tormented as a result of seeing things differently. One student struggled all quarter with why the gifted classes in her school were basically all White, asking me repeatedly in her journal if I thought this was statistically odd. Another wondered why at the end of the year her classroom teacher did not know that the African American girl she was tutoring could read some basic texts, and why she referred to the child as a nonreader. Many questioned why the readings and our discussions were making things harder instead of easier. This feeling remained despite our discussions on the importance of self-reflection in dealing with issues of diversity. The students in general were more willing at the end of the second quarter to reveal their internal struggles. One student captured what a few others were feeling: "I feel like I need to take more courses that force me to learn about kids who do not speak English well and other minorities, but I am at the end of my studies. What am I supposed to do?" A number of students admitted that they had hoped that their exposure to different ways of looking at learning would provide them with quick and clear answers. Instead, they struggled to define the difficult steps needed to successfully teach all of their students.

Learning to teach all students is a lifelong endeavor. Some members of our class wanted continuing focus on issues of social change. They are committed to developing a deeper understanding that will result in more enlightened pedagogy. Many of these students individually contacted me after the second course ended. They seem especially concerned with how to address diversity when they have a position. Implicit in their request to continue the dialogue via e-mail is the need to make this critical conversation an ongoing part of their professional development.

REFERENCES

Barrera, R. (1992). The cultural gap in literature-based literacy instruction. *Education and Urban Society, 24*(2), 227–243.

Delpit, L. (1988). The silenced dialogue: Power and pedagogy in educating other people's children. *Harvard Educational Review, 58,* 280–298.

Delpit, L. (1995). *Other people's children.* New York: New Press.

Diamond, B., & Moore, M. (1995). *Multicultural literacy: Mirroring the reality of the classroom.* White Plains, NY: Longman.

hooks, b. (1994). *Teaching to transgress.* New York: Routledge.

Ladson-Billings, G. (1994). *The dreamkeepers: Successful teachers of African American children.* San Francisco: Jossey-Bass.

Narayan, K. (1991). According to their feelings: Teaching and healing with stories. In C. Witherell & N. Noddings (Eds.), *Stories lives tell: Narrative and dialogue in education* (pp. 113–135). New York: Teachers College Press.

Paley, V. G. (1979). *White teacher.* Cambridge, MA: Harvard University Press.

Reyes, M. (1992). Challenging venerable assumptions: Literacy instruction for linguistically different students. *Harvard Educational Review, 62,* 427–446.

Sleeter, C. (1994). White racism. *Multicultural Education, 1,* 5–39.

Willis, A. I. (1997). Exploring multicultural literature as cultural production. In T. Rogers & A. Soter (Eds.), *Reading across cultures: Teaching literature in a diverse society* (pp. 135–160). New York: Teachers College Press.

PART III

Students' Rights and Responsibilities in Making Decisions About Their Own Learning

Team Meetings, Integrated Curriculum, and Literature Groups: Forums for Democratic Decision-Making

Suzanne S. McCotter

I WAS RAISED IN THE New York/New Jersey area, and came to the South with my husband, Keith, in an effort to find a change of pace and degree of independence. Teaching middle school was not part of my plan; with a secondary English education degree from Rutgers College, I fully intended to teach only high school, only English. We all know that job searches don't always cater to our whims, and I ended up—happily, as it turns out—teaching in a middle school. I became immersed in the challenges and opportunities of teaching and learning from young adolescents and now want to teach only middle school and never just one content area. I am working on a Ph.D. in Middle Grades Education, which keeps me current in the broader world of middle schools.

Education has always been valued above almost anything else in my family. My mother spent many years on the Board of Education in my hometown, and enthusiasm for school and learning was consistently expected and encouraged in our home. My father has been involved in progressive education for his entire career, first as a teacher and now as a principal. Most of what I learned about education has been through observation in his schools and challenging conversations with him. My own avocations have always involved reading, learning, and thinking. Adventures in my classrooms are often inspired by writers like Ted Sizer or Nancie Atwell. Helping kids develop passions like mine is part of what I hope I do as a teacher. (And a parent—I have to admit to a certain glee when my very active toddler brings me a book to read instead of a ball to throw.)

Growing up in an almost all-White, middle-class, rural Northern town, my experience with people from other cultures and backgrounds was minimal. Although I was from a liberal, accepting family, my knowledge of multicultural, socioeconomic, and race issues was intellectual and superficial. During college I made a conscious effort to take classes and gain experiences that would take me out of my narrow frame of reference. I took several literature classes—"The Black Novel," "Black Women Writers," and "Intro to Black Literature"—and was part of a leadership group that focused on issues of racism, sexism, and heterosexism. "Race and Rutgers," a history of race relations at Rutgers University, was the most significant course. We had lively discussions about current racial issues at the school; the majority of the class (including me) refused to take the final exam because institutional racism was still so prevalent. Nevertheless, I do not believe that I had gained a deep understanding of racism.

As a White Northerner, I had the "privilege" of not thinking about my race unless I chose to consider it. When I moved to Georgia, I came as an enlightened Northerner who could bring some truth to the people I was going to educate. What I found out was that I had never dealt with the issue of race, and that I had come from a place that was not only as racist as my new home, but much more hypocritical. Legislated integration in Southern counties has forced Southerners to deal with the issue of race. The township school systems in the North allow local communities to have a small all-White school two miles away from a small all-Black school, with obviously different and inequitable programs. Jonathan Kozol pointed out the correlational economic issues in *Savage Inequalities* (1992), and demonstrated fundamental reasons for changing the system. However, I saw little motivation or encouragement for change. While it is clear that racism does exist in the South, I will argue that both hypocrisy and racism exist in the North. With these experiences and observations, I joined the LEADS group and simultaneously began a new professional challenge.

BUILDING A SCHOOL AND CLASSROOM COMMUNITY

After teaching 8th grade for two years, I made a difficult transition to a new school, a new teaching partner (Sara Glickman), and a new grade level. The principal who opened this new school was committed to democracy as a practice and as a goal; we discussed shared decision-making and governance, along with grouping practices and issues of access and creating equal opportunity for all students. She had been principal of an elementary school with a predominantly African American, predominantly low-SES student body; many of the families from that school chose for their children to follow her to that middle school. The school is located in a rural area of predominantly white, middle-class families. As a result, we have a diverse population of students, and creating one community was a challenge.

Committed to involving parents, students, and community members in building that community, we invited them to share their opinions and dreams in a series of meetings the summer before the school opened. We worked together to develop common values for the school, a mission statement, and a decision-making process that involves staff, parents, and children. The Steering Committee read about different models of shared decision-making in schools (Glickman, 1993; Levin, 1991), and we agreed on a model that met our unique needs. The evolution of our school contributed greatly to the conversations that Sara and I had as we contemplated how to develop our 6th-grade team as a democratic classroom. We joined LEADS for support and ideas from others committed to social justice and democratic education.

Acknowledging the presence of racism and the need to deal with it overtly and honestly was one of the things Sara and I considered as we began to plan our team. We spent a lot of time talking about philosophy and "issues." Teams of teachers that work well together have to learn about each other before they can make productive decisions about their teaching. Our shared reading included Lisa Delpit's *Other People's Children* (1995), which gave us food for thought about the power of standard language and hearing all voices, essential for us as White female teachers of a half-African American school. We also read Deborah Meier's *The Power of Their Ideas* (1995), about Central Park East Secondary School, a successful high school in East Harlem and part of the Coalition of Essential Schools. My father was the director of that school at the time and Sara had visited it the year before, so we both had some familiarity with the school, but came away from the book with renewed interest in particular elements that we could use in our situation.

With some common background, Sara and I began to talk about goals for our team, ourselves, and our students. We were committed to building a community in which everyone had a voice. The team we envisioned was a place where students felt safe to learn, question, and grow. Our team needed to provide an environment where all students would be challenged and nurtured, by us and by one another. Open and honest communication with students, their parents, and each other was critical for us, as was really listening to our students. We wanted students to be rigorous about their learning; we valued assessment and proof of intellectual growth. And we wanted to have fun. The community we hoped to form should be a place where people wanted to be.

As a two-teacher middle school team, we had 45 to 50 students to teach. Who taught which students and in what order varied according to the units or projects on which we were working. From 9:15 A.M. until 12:30, all of our students were "on-team" for language arts, social studies, and science; math was after lunch. At 2:15, students had exploratory classes, and we had an hour and a half of planning time, which was critical to developing, discussing, and evaluating the elements in this chapter: team meetings, integrated curriculum projects, and literature groups.

TEAM MEETINGS

Sara had just finished a year observing other schools and talking with teachers both nationally and internationally, and proposed the idea of team meetings to meet the goals of building a community and upholding our democratic ideals of including student voices in all aspects of our team. There are many purposes for team meetings: to gain student input and feedback on curriculum, to discuss relevant social issues, or as an organization function for daily business and community news. Sara and I did not have a single goal for our daily meetings, except to get all students actively involved in the school community. We especially wanted to promote involvement from students who might not typically get the chance.

We developed a tentative format. Anyone who had a community issue could get it on the Team Meeting Agenda and bring it up. A student facilitator ran each meeting; a student recorder kept minutes. The format included places for "Thank Yous and Congratulations," "Announcements, Dates and Events," "Updates on Planning," "Old Business," "Problems/ Solutions," "New Business," and "Celebrations and Final Presentations." Because students raised issues important to them, they set the priorities, tone, and purpose of the meetings. Early issues included matters that we as teachers did not predict would be important, but that students found critical, such as having a back-flip contest or using the gym to play basketball.

The process started slowly. Sara and I modeled the first few meetings, and then student facilitators took over relatively smoothly. Crowd control, with 50 6th graders in a room, was a continuing problem; some facilitators tried to handle it, and students eventually supported each other better as Team Leaders. It also took considerable time to learn how to follow a problem or a proposal through to fruition. Initially, many problems or proposals died after they were brought up at Team Meeting. As teachers, we felt that it was important for the kids to take ownership of the issue and see it through themselves; as students, they waited for teachers to tell them what to do. We offered to act as adult sponsors, and advised the interested students to form a committee and set up a meeting, but committees rarely made a decision. Although the teachers were frustrated, the students did not seem to care about the lack of follow-through. Having brought up a problem, they let it go.

Toward the end of the year, the team developed a protocol for getting things done. The students put up sign-up sheets for committees, recruited adult sponsors, and held lunchtime meetings. As adult facilitators, we learned to ask directing questions without being directive. Do you have an adult sponsor? Have you set a meeting time? After working through a process, the students started to realize the potential of making decisions. Kesha brought up the problem that there was not time in the day for students to exercise, socialize, and relax. The team agreed that this was a problem. Her committee recommended forming a Walking Club. Interested students signed up at the beginning of each marking period, agreed to give up ten minutes of lunch time and follow club rules (like "no throwing rocks"), and walked around the building with an adult each day after lunch. The team Steering Committee organized sports banquets with awards every six weeks, kept a list of current members, and made sure rules were upheld.

T'annah and Jennifer noted that students playing Pencil Break (two children trying to break each other's pencils) was a community problem because the whole class got in trouble watching them. A Pencil Break committee decided that anyone playing Pencil Break had to pay a fine; the money would go toward buying classroom supplies. We didn't collect very much money, because as soon as the students started monitoring one another and holding each other accountable for community standards, Pencil Break stopped. The issue brought up the need for a judicial system, and the Pencil Break Committee became a Judicial Task Force.

When someone suggested a field trip, a committee immediately went into action. They brainstormed ideas, polled the team, and established priorities. Graciella and Shanna, being detail people, took over the office phone one day to find available dates, make reservations, and book a school bus. We spent a full day at Rock Eagle, a local 4-H camp, hiking up a mountain and doing facilitated team-building exercises.

Adults brought up issues as well. When there had been an "almost" fight on our team that had stopped because Will would not hit back, some of the other boys tormented him and called him a "wimp." The teachers took the opportunity to discuss the courage involved in walking away. It was an important discussion for the team to have, and Will was welcomed back into the community without any more name-calling.

Tricia Taylor (Chapter 10) had spent a lot of time observing in our classrooms, and Team Meetings were particularly interesting to her. She did a survey of the kids' perceptions of Team Meeting and found some who had problems with it. She posed this at Team Meeting and offered to sponsor a Team Meeting committee to look at the structure. This hard-working group came up with some great suggestions about how to revise our agenda by combining some items to eliminate confusion about when to bring things up, and to streamline the process. However, when this new and improved agenda was brought to the Team Meeting, the approval was underwhelming.

Latoya said, "No way—it's too confusing."

Lisa protested that "They can't change OUR Team Meeting!"

The students in the team had taken ownership of the Team Meeting and claimed it as *theirs*. Sara and I had thought the revised agenda a vast improvement—but we were only the authors and teachers.

Team meetings definitely empowered students to bring up issues important to them. A few weeks into school, Sara was involved in a conversation with a student who tended to be disruptive. Vicky said, "Ms. Glickman, I don't like you. I'm gonna get on the agenda and bring this up at Team Meeting!" The fact that she was angry at Sara was not as important as the fact that she saw Team Meeting as a productive place to get something done with her anger. (After a few seconds, she smiled and said, "Just kidding!")

CURRICULUM DECISIONS

Interestingly, students attributed all areas in which they had a voice to the Team Meeting process. They remember curriculum decisions, assessment, and exhibitions of work as having been a part of the Team Meetings, although they were not. Team Meeting was a small part of our day; however, we also wanted students to contribute to other learning decisions. James Beane (1993) has written eloquently about middle school curriculum and the need for students to have a voice in determining what should be included in it. His challenge is that "the curriculum must include possibilities for all views to be heard and for the presence of all people to be recognized" (p. 64). Because Georgia has a state-mandated curriculum, there is not a lot of leeway in what we teach. However, we can make decisions about how we approach it, what we do with it, and how it is assessed, and it is here that students have a voice.

Democratizing Group Processing

Since I expect students to work in groups all year (and for the rest of their lives), I commit several weeks at the beginning of each year to a unit on "Group Processing." Often, when I talk about this to colleagues who haven't had success with group work in their classrooms, they object that they couldn't possibly take three weeks away from their content; however, I have found that any content can be addressed while teaching kids how to work in groups. This year, we did group work using maps and geography as our basis, but it could easily have been done with math logic problems, scientific experiments, or poetry.

The essence of group processing is that groups need to recognize the problems that can keep them from getting their task done and set a goal to avoid it. For example, middle-schoolers are intensely interested in what their peers are doing, and they want to be physically active. Setting a goal to "get our work done" is not specific enough for a 6th grade group; they need to set a goal such as "we won't talk to anyone else in the classroom except our group until our work is done," or "we need the whole group's permission before we can get out of our seats." Setting group goals and assessing them at the end of a group task requires practice, but by the end of the year, the kids were really good at it. They could look around their group and say, "We are a group who loves sports. No one is allowed to talk about basketball until the job is finished." Everyone is responsible for monitoring the conversation until the end, and that supervision is much more effective and efficient than mine.

Another integral part of group processing is determining group composition. This is an area where many middle school teachers hesitate because of the intense socializing that goes on among students of this age. The practical logic goes something like this: If they choose their own groups, they will choose to be with their friends and won't get their work done; if I assign them to groups, they will not be with people they are close friends with, and will get their work done. Actually, I've found that kids who do not choose their own groups are just as likely *not* to do their work as kids who have chosen their groups. There are different kinds of problems—kids refuse to work with people they don't like, or one child will ignore the rest of the group and do all the work. That is not to say that groups determined solely on the basis of friendship work well all the time, just that in my experience kids do better when they have some choice.

We've used several different strategies to work on how the groups are composed. The most obvious groups were based on interest. When we were doing a timeline of modern European history, the whole class read the chapters in our textbook, looked at the resources from the school and public libraries, and heard a short introduction to each topic we were going to study. They then wrote down (individually) the three topics that were most interesting to them, and a brief rationale for why they should be in that group. Looking at their expressed interests gave us a way to put students in groups that were interest-based, rather than with groups of friends.

Another way to give students choice while exercising some control over the group composition is to set up criteria for the groups. On the first day of school I asked students to look around the room and describe the class to me. The obvious characteristics that they come up with are that there are both boys and girls in the class and there was more than one race in the class. I asked them to form groups of four on that first day that were representative of our class, with both genders, and more than one race. Since cliques of children in our school tend to be single-gender and single-race, this broke up some of the groups. It also helped set the tone for our team, that we were all going to work together.

After I gained the trust of the students, one of the most effective ways to form groups was to ask the students to be honest about people with whom they worked well. I set the stage by talking about how much I needed their honest opinions, and assured them that no one else would ever see what they wrote down. I then walked them through the following four questions:

1. What are some things you do very well when you work in groups?
2. What are some things you don't do well in groups?
3. Look around the room and write down 3–4 people you think you work well with.
4. The last question is very private, so be very sure no one else sees your paper, and fold it up when you are done. Who are some people in this room that you know you don't do a good job when you are in a group with them? These may be close friends of yours, or they may be people you like very much, but they are people who you know you do not work with well when you are in a group on this team.

I have never failed to be amazed at the honesty and maturity with which children answer these questions. It lets me show them that I return their trust, and gives them an opportunity to have some power over whom they will work with.

Of course, there are always problems that come with group work. Some days we had to stop and go back to individual work because things got out of control. Sometimes a student didn't work well even after several group changes and that individual needed to be a "group of one" for a while. However, Sara and I believed that working well in groups was a lifelong priority and worth teaching the children.

Democratic communities don't just happen. They take planning, hard work, and practice. Teaching my students how to work and live in a democratic community has been essential to building it. Pate, Homestead, and McGinnis (1997), in their book about a middle school team, noted that "teaching about the democratic process is not the same as experiencing the democratic process" (p. 15). Through group processing, students begin to develop the skills essential to the democratic process of making decisions.

Democratizing Curriculum Development

The content to be covered in our curriculum was very broad. For example, 6th grade social studies includes the history and geography of Europe, the Middle East, and Africa from ancient to modern times. The magnitude and scope of that is a bit overwhelming. We tried to focus on areas and issues that were important to our students, and that gave them an understanding of other cultures and ways of life.

Our first unit involved ancient Egypt. We gathered resources, developed background knowledge, and encouraged the kids to become immersed in Egypt. Then we asked them what they wanted to do with that information. Our decision came not from a social studies discussion of ancient Egypt, but a conversation about a science fiction short story about schools of the future. Discussing what schools would be like in the future evolved into a discussion about what they had liked about schooling in the past. Some students recalled their elementary school experiences with MicroSociety; they had created a town, complete with economy, jobs, and judicial system.

Our *Egyptian MicroSociety* was born. Students took on roles including scribe, priest, farmer, and slave; they invited our principal to act as Pharaoh. They learned hieroglyphics, made models of Egyptian games, planned and produced an Egyptian banquet, developed a burial ritual, and made costumes and jewelry. As the time came to perform the microsociety simulation, we were also faced with moving from our temporary building to a new facility. The students really began to feel ownership of the new grounds when we had to find a site for the Nile Valley. The simulation became a celebration of what we had learned and how far we had come—in location and as a learning community.

As we finished Egypt and moved on to ancient Greece, the students thought and wrote about how to demonstrate what they were learning. Sara and I wanted them to share their knowledge with the broader school community. As I read their responses, it seemed that a lot of kids were interested in putting on a Greek play; they had read and learned about Greek theater. But when I asked the team for their ideas, my project never even got mentioned. The students came up with the wonderful idea of a living museum. We invited other students to take a "Walk Through Ancient Greece," where they experienced the Olympics, a theatrical version of a Greek myth, a reenactment of a battle of the Trojan War, and renditions of Greek art, architecture, and writing.

Bringing our work to the next level of sharing it with the community increased the pride and excitement of the team. They wanted to be the best they could for their audience of peers and took ownership of their ideas. When they heard other students expressing a desire to do the same thing in their classes, they claimed it as their idea, but wrote down the steps they had taken and described the excruciatingly hard work and hours of practice that had gone into it.

I overheard Trey having a conversation in my classroom one day shortly after we'd finished our Ancient Greece project.

"I hate school!" he said in the vehement way 6th graders have.

"What do you mean, Trey? Tell me what you hate about school," I pressed him.

"Well," he said, "not everything, just social studies. I hate social studies."

"Did you hate what we did with Egypt?"

"No, that was OK," he grudgingly acknowledged.

"How about what we did with Ancient Greece?"

"That there, that was fun!" he said loudly and emphatically. "Can we do that when we study Africa?"

I have learned not to answer questions like that anymore, because what the students come up with will be better than what I could design, and it will be theirs. Our studies of Ancient Egypt and Greece went a long way toward the goals that Sara and I set. The students were actively involved, had learned content based on their interests, had worked together as a community, and certainly had fun doing it. We also increased our knowledge of democracy through our class conversations about the societies we were studying. Students were quick to point out the fallacies in referring to them as democracies: "What about the women?" "But I thought they had slaves!" Their understanding about democracy came about more from the processes of negotiation, planning, and working as committee members.

Students were also integrally involved in developing assessment tools. At the beginning of a project, the group (including me) discussed what a "good" project would include. Initially, the students awkwardly discussed criteria such as neat handwriting and spelling. After learning some vocabulary and deciding what they really thought was important, they became experts. Later assessment discussion involved shouts of "Style!", "Process!", and "Mechanics!", among others. Students struggled with the same issues as teachers; we had a recurring dialogue about whether to include Effort as a category. Some students proclaimed, "If the project is good, why does it matter how much time I spent on it?" while others maintained, "If I worked much harder than anyone else, shouldn't I get credit for that?"

Having a democratic classroom does not mean that I give up my position as the adult and the primary decision-maker in the room. I am constantly planning for and reflecting on what happens. When the children get overexcited the day before winter vacation, I am going to plan something calm. Inviting students to have a voice and choice in their learning has led to increased excitement about their learning and commitment to their community. It also means that I have to be very secure about my role as the teacher in that community.

I fully believe in the potential of students to make decisions and act as leaders. I also know that I have experience and expertise that they do not have. Part of my role as their teacher was to model leadership for them. We talked about the decisions that I made and why I made them. My students came to understand when they were going to be part of a decision and when they were not. While there remained tension between the ideal and reality, as the year progressed students developed increasing control over classroom events and processes because they honed their leadership and decision-making skills.

LITERATURE GROUPS, WRITING GROUPS, AND INCLUSIVE TEAMING

Many teachers struggle with the issue of ability grouping. Philosophic issues conflict with logistical ones, and societal opinions differ sharply. Ethically, Sara and I were committed to as little ability grouping as possible. The organization of our school and the philosophy and personalities of our colleagues allowed us to virtually eliminate "pullout" gifted and special education classes. Special education teacher Ann and gifted teacher

Melissa joined our team daily for language arts. They served students with diverse needs *in* the classroom, and the entire team benefited from their expertise. This inclusive teaming was especially important for the students whose needs, both for enrichment and support, were not formally identified. The lines between who was an "identified" special ed or gifted and who was not were blurred, and many *un*identified students lobbied for opportunities to go to those classrooms. This seemed to lessen the stigma or elitism often associated with pullout services.

Throughout the year, we frequently split the students up into literature groups. Sometimes the students chose the group; other times we placed them. Students chose which books they would read in a variety of ways, including having the adults "pitch" their books or genre. Melissa tended to sponsor groups that read more difficult books, and Ann focused on easier, high-interest books. Neither group, however, was automatically composed of particular populations. They shifted according to interests, needs, and personalities. It was not unusual for a child to be in my group one time, and the "gifted" group the next. In one literature group session, Melissa had two students in her group who would never be identified as gifted. Neither of them had exceptional test scores, nor were they particularly good writers, but they were avid readers. Melissa reported that they added a whole new dimension to discussions, from unique perspectives to contagious enthusiasm.

In one of the first literature groups, each participant read a different biography. Several chose sports figures. Anthony read the O. J. Simpson (1995) book *I Want to Tell You.* Simpson's trial was *the* news item at that time, and the conversation returned to the trial and issues of race frequently. Many of the students had stories to tell about race and how discrimination had affected them or their family members. One day they got into a conversation about Simpson's interracial marriage to Nicole Brown Simpson. The group, mostly Black males, all felt that it was absolutely wrong for Black people and White people to marry. They expressed disgust at the very idea.

The literature group's small size and high comfort level fostered honest conversation, with Sara (a European-American, female adult) listening and challenging their thinking. Students may not have changed their minds about issues as a result of the conversations, but they did hear other perspectives in a thought-provoking dialogue about an issue central to their lives. Morris, who kept protesting, "It's just not right," was futilely pushed to give some rationale for what he was saying. Anthony, who was reading the book, was in the habit of reading with his mother each night and then discussing it before writing in his response journal. He began to share some of his mother's comments in the group, and it was apparent that she wanted him to think more about issues of violence than about interracial marriage: "My mother says it doesn't matter what race they were, because Nicole's dead now."

A similar dialogue occurred later in the year as each literature group read *Shabanu* (Staples, 1989) to coincide with our study of the Middle East. *Shabanu* is the story of a young girl growing up and raising camels in the deserts of Pakistan. As the youngest daughter of a son-less family, Shabanu had been able to escape some of the traditional female responsibilities of her culture by helping with the camels. At the time of the story, she is coming into womanhood and is faced with the inevitability of an arranged marriage and relative loss of her family. Our guiding question for the book, "What forces have powers in Shabanu's life?", was important for our discussions of class, gender, environment, and age as powerful forces. We also examined and contrasted these forces with the forces that have power in our own lives.

Melissa and I were working together with 16 students, and were alternating the lead role. We were nervous about the maturity of the students and the adult topics in parts of the book, and we tried to approach them with as much integrity and honesty as we could. As we got to the passage in the book where Phulan, Shabanu's older sister, is almost attacked and taken as consort by the landlord's guests, we tried to prepare the students for it by explaining to them what was about to happen in the novel. They then had the option of reading by themselves or reading with me in the corner; most of them came to read with me. We had an animated conversation about the role of women and power in a Middle Eastern Muslim society, the similarities and differences in our society, and the related topic of date rape. Students who were reading by themselves drifted over and joined the conversation, which ranged from victim blaming to gender bias.

Referring to Phulan's plight, Kelly said, "Well, she shouldn't have been, you know, wiggling her hips." I looked around to see heads nodding. We first asked students to return to the text, where they found, instead of provocative or flirtatious behavior, a description of a young woman who was walking along the desert sand and who looked beautiful. We then had a forthright conversation about one of our favorite phrases—*what if?* What if she *had* been wiggling her hips? Would the landlord have been justified in his actions? This single conversation may not have changed the long-term point of view of any student sitting in that circle, but the discussion reinforced the notion that this classroom was a place where it was safe to explore issues that were relevant to our lives, as well as connected to our studies. We were all sorry when that discussion ended.

At the end of the year we applied the same structure we had used for literature groups to writing groups; each teacher sponsored a different kind of group, and students chose. Sara conducted a writing workshop for kids who had an individual piece or genre in mind. I sponsored a poetry group to read, write, and talk about poems. Melissa's group published a newspaper. Ann, due to the paperwork constraints of special education, did writing activities combined with Year-End Evaluations of identified special education students; they had a great experience, but those students were not able to choose their writing. Those writing groups led to some of the most enjoyable experiences we had all year, as well as some of the best products. My poetry group designed a Poetry Calendar that everyone could hang in their lockers the following year. Melissa's group learned a great deal about publication, layout, and salesmanship as they published two issues of their paper. In Sara's room, products ranged from Kristy's and Susan's letters from a Holocaust survivor to her American cousin (which they shared with us in social studies) to the piece David wrote about his native country of Korea, complete with faxed revisions from his father in Seoul.

Our commitment at the beginning of the year to hear students' voices manifested itself in a number of ways. At Team Meeting we discussed issues relevant to our school lives. Skills in group processing allowed everyone to be involved in curriculum and assessment decisions. Literature and writing groups allowed us to raise deeper, more difficult societal issues as they related to the books we read. Working to democratize the classroom means leaving behind a lot of the comfortable routines and standard decisions that help teachers feel in control. I would not trade that comfort level for the richer learning and heightened involvement students experience when they have a voice in making meaningful decisions. The key is making a philosophical commitment to sharing power with kids; the rest is following through, facilitating, and providing opportunities.

REFERENCES

Beane, J. A. (1993). *A middle school curriculum: From rhetoric to reality.* Columbus, OH: National Middle School Association.

Delpit, L. (1995). *Other people's children: Cultural conflict in the classroom.* New York: New Press.

Glickman, C. (1993). *Renewing America's schools: A guide for school-based reform.* San Francisco: Jossey-Bass.

Kozol, J. (1992). *Savage inequalities: Children in America's schools.* New York: Harper Perennial.

Levin, H. (1991). *Building school capacity for effective teacher empowerment: Applications to elementary schools with at-risk students.* New Brunswick, NJ: Center for Policy Reform in Education.

Meier, D. (1995). *The power of their ideas.* Boston: Beacon Press.

Pate, P. E., Homestead, E. R., & McGinnis, K. L. (1997). *Making integrated curriculum work: Teachers, students, and the quest for coherent curriculum.* New York: Teachers College Press.

Simpson, O. J. (1995). *I want to tell you.* Boston: Little Brown.

Staples, S. F. (1989). *Shabanu: Daughter of the wind.* New York: Alfred A. Knopf.

CHAPTER 9

Evolution

Sarah Johnson

THIS IS A STORY of change. It is the story of how my perspective on teaching changed and the story of how that altered standpoint
was enacted in my classroom. It is a story without an ending, for just as
evolution proceeds perpetually in the natural world, I, too, continue to
evolve as an educator, following a cycle of reading and learning new
concepts, applying them in the classroom, watching and listening to students, and reflecting on what has happened, which leads me right back
to the beginning of a new cycle.

CYCLE ONE: DEMOCRACY AS STUDENT CHOICE

Like so many instances of personal or professional growth, my initial
change was precipitated by an intense dissatisfaction. At that time I was
a special education teacher who spent Sunday mornings looking at Help
Wanted ads and Sunday evenings in a state of dread. I was a teacher
who approached her plan book as a mass of rectangles that needed to be
filled. Everything felt superficial. I knew that the students were most
often bored and unengaged, and that they were truly learning very little.
We were merely "playing school."

I worked with rural middle school students who had been identified as Mildly Intellectually Disabled. This means that at some point in their school careers they experienced a prolonged period of "failure," of not being able to do what was expected of them. They had difficulty with language. They didn't process, or they didn't decode, or they didn't catch on to the patterns of "standard" English. These students spent their elementary years in very regimented, basal-oriented classrooms. When they didn't "succeed," they were put in settings in which skills were even more fragmented, in classrooms that were populated only with other students who had similar school histories, in classrooms that were often located away from their regular education age peers.

At this time I heard about a way of teaching with which my spirit resonated, a way of teaching that respected learners and teachers, a way of teaching that many refer to as whole language. As I read journal articles and took a short course, I came to believe that my classroom could metamorphose into one like those I studied, permeated with a genuine sense of purpose and alive with learners working enthusiastically to gain knowledge that was of value to them.

The first cycle of study, change, and reflection was launched. Prior to these professional learning experiences I believed that the skill-and-drill curriculum that had been preferred by my administrators must really be best for students, even though I felt uncomfortable with it and I saw that students were not benefiting from it. I believed that the problem was my inability to keep checklists of vocabulary mastered or skills demonstrated. Other teachers who had struck out on their own to remedy the same problems I witnessed strengthened my conviction that I needed to try something new. Our school had a new principal that year who was supportive of the whole language movement. Her encouragement through faculty meetings and in-service training sessions was crucial.

"What do you want to know about?" That was the question on the board one morning when the students entered the room, rather than the more typical workbook page assignments for each reading group. The students talked to each other, made individual lists, and finally worked as a whole class to select a topic of study. Our first discovery quest was "castles."

That evening I visited the public library and checked out all the books I could find that had anything to do with castles. I brought informational books and picture books. I brought books about knights and dragons and armor. We visited our school library and found more books. Shirley found a book about food during medieval times and Michael found a book that had a diagram of all the parts of a castle.

Soon the students were spread about the room, at the table, on the floor, in little circles of desks pulled together; the classroom was alive with the sounds of discovery. Students called out ideas for projects and shared exciting finds with their friends. It was a welcome relief from the hollow, empty room that had existed just two days before, blank faces obediently staring at the chalkboard or workbook. Minds were active, wondering, questioning. Students wrote stories, made posters, and extended their vocabularies. Each student planned a project and pursued learning that was of personal interest. Michael and Keith worked together to make a poster that showed the parts of a castle. Tiffany wrote a short play about a princess and a knight and enlisted Shirley and Patrick to help her perform it. The students kept reading logs of the picture books they read, including title, author information, and a brief comment on the difficulty level of each book, which gave them their first experience with self-evaluation.

The changes I made in the direction of creating a whole language classroom have a tangible connection to the goal of education for democracy. Patrick Shannon (1993) describes a democracy as a system in which people participate meaningfully in decisions that affect their lives. In a democratic classroom students are participating meaningfully in decisions ranging from selecting criteria for grading to determining what knowledge is produced.

While these practices don't overtly tackle the big questions of systems of domination (Edelsky, 1994), they do create the necessary blueprint for taking charge and shaping systems and events that affect their lives. I can't imagine that students like mine who had long been conditioned not to question or challenge—to in fact believe that the existing imbalance of power is just the way things are—could ever suddenly wake up and be fully aware of systems of domination and consequently resolve to challenge them. My students had been the victims of both social and educational systems that denied them choices. I wanted to teach them that they had some control over their lives and could make important decisions.

I knew that the changes I had made in the classroom were ones made in the right direction, and that I was unwilling to ever let things revert to the state that had precipitated those changes. However, I felt as though I was flying blind, and I was not sure I could adequately defend the practices I had begun to implement with anything other than statements about enthusiasm and joy in learning. What would happen when it was time to take the end-of-the-book test? I wanted to make radical changes, but I wanted to know that I was fulfilling my obligation to the students. I began a new cycle of learning by entering graduate school.

CYCLE TWO: DEMOCRACY AS QUESTIONING SOCIAL INSTITUTIONS

I was most excited by the "big picture" nature of the whole language movement. I was excited to find educators who looked beyond mastery test scores as the ends we sought. This orientation toward helping students understand, critique, and then shape the world in which we live was emphasized in my first course in graduate school. In a literature course entitled "Guiding the Reading of Children," Joel Taxel helped me become aware of the social messages implicit and explicit in children's literature. Painfully, I came to see how my own education in the South in the 1960s had served to reinforce the status quo of racial inequities past and present. He read us *Nettie's Trip South* (Turner, 1987), set during slavery. I was stunned. I was immediately rocketed back to Miss Harris's 4th-grade class in my elementary school outside Atlanta. I remembered asking about how the slaves were treated and being assured that they were treated very well and were happy being taken care of. I also remembered knowing that I was allowing myself to believe a lie because doing so made life easier and less painful. At that moment I knew viscerally, not just intellectually, the power that education wields in either promulgating or remediating social injustices. I came to see not only the manner in which the classroom was structured, but the content of the literature as essential to providing an education that promoted within students the desire to question the world as they found it and to propose better ways of living.

Focusing on social justice helped me reconcile the woman I was with the teacher I wanted to be. This woman sitting at the teacher's desk was more than a frustrated teacher—she was a person who had Convictions and Beliefs. She was a person who had tried to stop bulldozers from converting a treasured wood into tract housing at age four, a person who had read Thoreau's *Essay on Civil Disobedience* and then helped her high school classmates learn how to avoid the draft during the Vietnam "conflict," a person who had become a vegetarian rather than support factory farming practices. I wanted that woman to be my teacher self, too.

The invitation to join the LEADS group launched me full force into making social justice the core of our classroom study. At our meetings, we spent hours discussing the tie between literacy education and democracy. As Carole Edelsky points out, "Despite secret ballots and slogans like 'majority rules,' we don't have a democracy . . . In a system where corporations are so privileged that they can write the laws as well as decide which laws they'll obey, you can't have a democracy" (1994, pp. 252–253). These words struck home for me. Past experiences with environmental groups had made me acutely aware of the flaws in the system, especially the undue influence corporations have in Congress. I saw a possible point of connection between classroom work and citizen action, and a direct link between literacy education and democracy.

I reasoned that in order for citizens to actively and effectively pursue changes in laws and policies that are unjust, they must first realize that some laws are created out of self-interest rather than from more altruistic motives. I also knew that passion fuels the work needed to evoke change through grassroots movements. Even though I knew that the questioning and challenging nature of such movements was an American tradition, I felt timid about using the public school classroom as a training ground for such action during this period of close public scrutiny of what some labeled the "liberal agenda" in education.

At this time I read *A Pedagogy for Liberation* by Ira Shor and Paulo Freire (1987). Its message called me to take another step toward becoming the teacher I wanted to be, a teacher who met each day with goals greater than merely preparing students to pass a written test. When I read Ira Shor's words, "A big crisis now in the U.S. is student resistance to the official curriculum. Another way of putting it is that teachers and administrators are refusing to change the curriculum that alienates students" (p. 5). I knew the answer to the eternal question asked in every teacher's lounge, "Why won't they try? Why won't they pay attention? They act like they just don't care." As Shor explained, " . . . motivation has to be inside the action of study itself, inside the students' recognition of the importance of knowing to them" (p. 5). I saw the utter absurdity of those "motivating activities" I had been taught to provide at the beginning of a lesson.

I read Paulo Freire's discussion on the dichotomization of the two moments of the cycle of knowledge: the moment in which new knowledge is produced and the moment in which that knowledge is perceived:

> Knowledge is produced in a place far from the students, who are asked only to memorize what the teacher says. Consequently, we reduce the act of knowing the existing knowledge into a mere transference of the existing knowledge. And the teacher becomes just the specialist in transferring knowledge. Then, he or she loses some of the necessary, the indispensable qualities which are demanded in the production of knowledge, as well as in knowing the existing knowledge. Some of those qualities are, for example, action, critical reflection, curiosity, demanding inquiry, uneasiness, uncertainty—all these virtues are indispensable to the cognitive subject, to the person who learns. (in Shor & Freire, 1987, p. 8)

Although I didn't initially comprehend the message fully, something made me reread it until I grasped it. I knew that this was something I wanted to have as an intrinsic part of me when I went into the classroom each day.

I searched for something to thoroughly engage the students, something to really capture their interest, something that would trigger the questioning and thinking that I knew my six Black and two White students were capable of. I thought about what they had responded to in a big way in our readings so far. *Aunt Harriet's Underground Railroad in the Sky* (Ringgold, 1992) had evoked a lot of interest and some questions. I thought about my strong reaction to hearing *Nettie's Trip South*. We studied slavery as an unjust legal institution and learned about those who had worked against it. We examined the reality that laws are sometimes passed in the interest of the few with harsh consequences for others from the safety of historical distance.

I began by reading *Nettie's Trip South* aloud to my own students and asking them to write a response. I was reassured by Shor that "What matters most to me in the beginning is how much and how fast I can learn about the students . . . I fly by the seat of my pants a lot without a fully architected course plan or reading list to reassure me with familiar order." It was that freedom that enabled us, one teacher and eight so-called mentally handicapped students, to find our own truths when we investigated slavery.

Things did not always go perfectly. Even though I had reached a level of intellectual understanding that it was professionally acceptable to invent as we went along, I struggled with deeply internalized feelings of concern about not being "in charge" or not "doing my job." Some afternoons I would feel weighed down by thoughts like, "Tameka and Chandra didn't know what they were reading." Or, if products attempted that day weren't of the caliber I had hoped for, I would slip into a negative internal dialogue and tell myself, "I'm just wasting their time." Usually I would catch myself and turn this pattern of thinking around. Instead of letting myself off the hook by saying, "They don't . . . " or "They can't . . . ," I tried to avoid what Delpit called the "litany of deficit" (1994). So instead I asked, "How can we . . . ?"

And we did. We questioned at the most basic level, to try and understand what we read. The students chose which books they wanted to read and worked in small groups with partners they selected themselves. They helped each other read and discover meaning. I had written their learning goals for this activity on a piece of construction paper: to learn as much as possible about slavery, and to think of and ask important questions.

I moved from group to group with the sign in hand and asked, "How are you doing on these goals?" Students showed me their written notes detailing the conditions of slavery. Where were the questions? These young people had noted deplorable living conditions (Chad wrote, "They didn't even get pants to wear," from reading David Adler's biography of Frederick Douglass) and gross violations of basic human rights (Tameka and Chandra had written, "You can't even have a real wedding with a preacher"), but they had not written any questions.

I worked from what they were doing well to push them to new levels of critical thinking. To prompt questions, I said, "I know this seems hard because you aren't quite sure what I mean and you haven't had much practice doing things like this before." As I spoke I could see the endless parade of the kind of writing these students had done, copying from the board, "Today is Tuesday. Tomorrow is Wednesday. We will have hot dogs for lunch." I asked students to report on their progress toward the two goals. Several students volunteered information that met goal one. I observed that we seemed to be stuck on goal two, thinking of and asking important questions. So I put this quote from Faith Ringgold (1992) on the board: "It was against the law for a slave to learn to read or write." When the students remained silent I commented, "Well, this is an interesting fact. Let's see . . . notice that it doesn't say the slaves weren't able to learn to read and write. It just says they weren't allow—" Chad cut me off.

"I've got a question. Why weren't the slaves permitted to learn to read?"

"Amen," I encouraged. "This young man can ask a question." As I wrote Chad's question on the board, Tim spoke up.

"I know. If they could read, they might get a book that would tell them how to get out of there."

Yes, as Carole Edelsky so wisely stated, "Re-theorizing language education to make it serve education *for* democracy means highlighting the relationship between language and power" (1994, p. 255).

We dared to ask a question. From that first query came many more. We questioned the thinking of people living at that time. We questioned what quality of human nature would enable brave souls to battle fearlessly against a Goliath foe. We questioned ourselves and asked what we would have done had we lived in those times. We dared to name institutionalized domination in this land of the free. Even though our country has officially tidied up the unsightly blemish of slavery, I felt that encouraging my students to question the law was risky business. In my more anxious moments, I pictured Phyllis Schlafly lurking outside my classroom door. She never showed.

We reached and stretched academically. We took notes from a video and posed more questions for class discussion. We read biographies of abolitionists and taught classmates about the person we had studied. We made a timeline of key events pertaining to slavery in the United States.

These products and presentations were not flawless. But by trying really hard work, by being supported by teacher and classmates, by being encouraged to stretch and think and act in ways never before asked of them in the classroom, these students surpassed any previous academic level of achievement. They read more widely, wrote more extensively, and discussed more thoughtfully. I also believe their self-images took on new dimensions.

I was learning, too. I learned that the salient question is not only what issues to tackle, but also the manner in which the issue is addressed. Teaching to support democracy meant teaching in a way that develops the understanding that "ordinary people make a difference in shaping events" (Peterson, 1994). I wrote in my teaching journal how I hoped to translate Peterson's words into classroom practice:

> Have the students find an issue that is relevant to their daily lives and pursue it with relentless vigor. Modify the traditional "who, what, when, where, why" to get to the real questions: Who bene-fits? Who suffers? Who promotes? What are the results to different segments of society? When was the policy instituted? When was it challenged? When did it happen in terms of the political-cultural scene? Where are those directly in charge of promulgating the con-dition at hand? Why do certain people support it? Why do certain people oppose it?
>
> Remember the words of Gloria Ladson-Billings (1994), "Tell-ing isn't teaching." Let "What do you think?" and "How could you find out?" become watchwords.

Sometimes I fretted about not doing enough, not going deep enough or fast enough. But I realized that such thinking is counterproductive, and people need time to assimilate such radical changes in being. I believe that while there is much to do, so many dragons to slay, we can't let the magnitude of the task render us so impatient that we fail to recognize the steps the students (and ourselves) are making toward the goal. Shor advises:

> If teachers don't think in terms of phases, levels, and gradations in a long process of change, they may fall into a paralyzing trap of saying that every-thing must be changed at once or it isn't worth trying to change anything at all. (in Shor & Freire, 1987, p. 35)

So I try to be patient with myself and with my students, and to realize that we are making progress, we are moving toward our goal. Each increment of democratizing the classroom brings us one step closer.

CYCLE THREE: STUDENTS WRITING THEIR OWN IEPS

The next step took us from curriculum to assessment. Each spring I develop an Individual Education Plan (IEP) for each student in accordance with Public Law 94-142. Typically, the entire process from review of progress made during the current year to the setting of goals and objectives for the coming year is done entirely by the teacher. Parents who attend meetings are offered the opportunity to contribute to the plan. However, the subject of the plan, the student, is rarely given an opportunity to play a meaningful role in this process. In fact, students are often left unaware of the content of the plans that have been developed for them and serve merely as couriers of papers to be signed.

Each spring I also hear disgruntled comments from my students. "Why can't I take regular classes? Why won't you·let me out of special ed? What am I going to take next year? Are you going to be my teacher again?" The voices uttering these questions are full of frustration. They convey a feeling of being powerless to shape their own futures. These anxious comments have nagged at my conscience for a number of years, but now I was unable to dismiss them.

I wondered what would happen if these disgruntled students, who are labeled Mildly Intellectually Disabled and Learning Disabled, sat down with me and participated in the entire process of developing their own IEPs. Would taking part in this process assuage their feelings of victimization? Would they be capable of giving meaningful input into the writing of this document?

Once again, I followed the pattern of reading and reflecting before I embarked on a new endeavor. I needed to ground my thinking. I needed affirmation that what I wanted to do was sound educational practice.

Mary Peters (1990) stated that although special education students are rarely thought to have the right to be an active participant on the IEP team, this right is stipulated in PL 94-142. She argued, " . . . when they are empowered as active team members in all aspects of the IEP process, students have an opportunity to increase their independence, self-advocacy skills, and self-esteem" (p. 32). In her book *Teaching to Transgress* (1994), bell hooks describes teaching as a practice of freedom if one teaches "without reinforcing existing systems of domination" (p. 18), and Freire pointed out that "dialogue is a challenge to existing domination" (in Shor & Freire, 1987, p. 99).

Although I had found professional support in these authors, I worried about the students' ability to assess their strengths and weaknesses, and that they might suggest goals and objectives that were inappropriate in my eyes. So the class participated in several activities to prepare us for this intensive work. I interviewed each individually to determine the students' perceptions of the IEP process, their opinions on their current school situation, and their overall goals for school and life beyond school.

All the students indicated a general understanding of what the IEP was about; however, only two of the students realized that teachers were the ones who made most of the decisions. One student was quite outspoken about being included in the IEP writing process. He said, "I came last year in Ms. Davis's room and I saw that yellow paper on what I'm going to learn about. I think kids ought to get involved 'cause we're doing the work. We're growing up, so let us know what is going on."

Next, students rated themselves on 17 student behaviors and specific academic skills about which I had knowledge of their current functioning level. At the end of the survey, students listed strengths and areas that needed development. Their response showed me that they knew themselves quite well.

I selected Quint for the first IEP because I had taught him in some capacity since he was in first grade. He was also the most outspoken about being involved. We began with the standardized testing data, since this was the method I used to help myself get oriented when writing IEPs. When I showed him his scores on the Wide Range Achievement Test 3 (WRAT-3), he immediately put his head down on the desk. His grade equivalent on the reading subtest was grade 4. We then discussed the nature of the test (reading words in isolation). I pulled some of the books off the shelf that he had read and showed him that the reading level of those books was grade 6. He was somewhat mollified by this new information.

In analyzing his learning needs, Quint told me that he did not always put forth his full effort and that he had trouble paying attention when there were distractions in the room. We then set long-term goals and their concomitant short-term objectives. He immediately stated that he wanted to read at a higher level. When I asked what activities he thought would help him reach this goal, he stated that he needed to read more and read harder books. I helped him phrase these as traditional objectives. He also indicated that he needed to practice reading words in isolation since he would take the same test (WRAT-3) again next year, so we wrote an objective stating he would have weekly lists of 10 words on which he would have lessons on dividing into syllables and would read the list to the teacher each week.

The next long-term goal that he set was to become a better student. I asked him what behaviors would show that he had become a better student. He listed doing a careful job on all projects and major assignments (he had had several problems related to this very thing during the year), having a serious attitude in class (he had listed "stop acting" and "get serious" as areas that he needed to develop on the self-assessment survey), and participating in lessons by asking questions and volunteering to give answers. He further refined these statements when describing the criteria for mastery.

When I asked what his goals for written expression were, he was unsure. I said that he should think of what kind of writing would help him with other goals that he had for his life. I reminded him that during the initial interview he indicated that he enjoyed learning about race relations and wanted to pursue this interest and study Black history when he finished high school. I suggested that we could think of the type of writing he would need for this pursuit. He thought he should learn to take notes from books and write reports about what he read.

Quint was very serious and thoughtful during the time we worked together. We began our work on Friday afternoon, but we were not able to finish in one session. He came by my room Monday morning to remind me we had to finish writing his IEP that afternoon. I judged his goals and his objectives to be appropriate; he set high but realistic criteria of mastery, and he was pragmatic in determining the method of evaluation for each objective. In other words, he did an excellent job of what some authors (Lovitt, Cushing, & Stump, 1994) found that most teachers did not do: he created a highly individualized, practical, and functional IEP. He also supported Peters's (1990) belief that "students may be able to offer insightful perceptions and valuable contributions to the IEP process in developing appropriate programs" (p. 33).

CYCLE FOUR: DEMOCRATIC PRACTICE REFINED

The nature of this cycle is quite different from that of the three cycles described above. This was a time of immersion in the theories and philosophies that underlie classroom practice. Through readings and discussions in a course entitled "Education As Democracy" taught by Carl Glickman, my understanding of the nature of democracy underwent further refinement, as did my vision of the link between literacy education and democracy.

My conception of democracy as I entered this class centered around individual rights and protection from exploitation by both government and private institutions. I thought of citizen participation in terms of righting a wrong. However, I began seeing democracy as an ongoing and integral part of citizenship that is not limited to interaction with a governmental agency, but functions daily in our communities and our classrooms. The meanings of the words *participation, obligation,* and *community* took on new dimensions.

Democracy is a system of living together, not solely a style of government. It is a way of living in community with others and living in a way that demonstrates respect, tolerance of differences, and equality of opportunity. The obligation is participation in its day-to-day workings in the classroom, workplace, neighborhood, town, and on to the macro-governmental level. The nature of the participation is largely dialogue. In a democracy, we must agree to disagree. So in a democratic classroom we must invite discussion and sincerely listen to the other members of our communities. We must listen with an open mind, but as we do, we need to be fully cognizant of the democratic values of liberty, freedom, and equality so that the product of these dialogues moves us closer to the ideal.

Moving closer to an ideal that is not yet realized brings to mind the failures of American democracy. However, hope is also part of our unique American democracy. In *An Aristocracy of Everyone*, Benjamin Barber explained:

> The language of universal citizenship as the common denominator of Americanism . . . is contradicted everywhere and in every American epoch by prejudice, discrimination, exclusion, inequality, and economic exploitation. Yet the use of a radically non exclusionary language anchored in universalist rhetoric—men are born equal, we the people, equality of rights—helped many groups originally excluded . . . preserve their hope and thus enabled them to mobilize political institutions that in time helped them win genuine suffrage. (Barber, 1992, p. 65)

Public education is a critical vehicle if that hope is to be realized. My readings and dialogue were now prompting me to think in broader terms, moving beyond my own classroom to ask, "What are schools for?" Education law professor John Dayton wrote that "in a democracy the fundamental purpose of public education is preparation for free citizenship and responsible democratic participation through education in democratic principles, and that education in democratic principles has utilitarian, humanitarian, and egalitarian benefits for individuals in the community" (1995, p. 137). Dayton's interpretation is not revolutionary. Thomas Jefferson justified the creation of public schools as a means of protecting ourselves from tyranny, with the purpose of illuminating the minds of "the people at large," and providing them with the historical perspective and knowledge essential "to know ambition under all its shapes, and prompt to exert their natural powers to defeat its purposes" (Jefferson, 1984, p. 365).

Still, I worried that preparing students for participation in democracy was somehow in conflict with the more academic goals of today's schools. One of my most profound learnings was that there is "no dichotomy between democracy and excellence . . . " (Barber, 1992, p. 13). The best example of education that overtly promotes democracy and academic excellence was provided at the Central Park East Schools. Principal Deborah Meier (1995) asked the same questions I had asked:

> Why were the self confident voices I knew so well at home and on the playground muted in the schools I taught in . . . ? I knew that human beings are by nature generators of ideas, what I didn't understand was how it was that some children recognized the power of their ideas while others became alienated from their own genius. How did schools, in small and unconscious ways, silence these persistent playground intellectuals? Could schools, if organized differently, keep this nascent power alive, extend it, and thus make a difference in what we grow up to be? The constraints that poverty and racism impose on the lives of children might be real, but could schools loosen rather than tighten them? (p. 3)

The second question my reading and thinking about democracy led me to ask was, Is it possible for schools to teach for democracy and address more conventional school goals at the same time? This question is also addressed by Meier: "It turns out that ideas are not luxuries gained at the expense of the 3 R's, but instead enhance them" (p. 4). As I read the many compelling examples of this statement, I came to believe with Meier (1995) that "public schools, in new and different forms, are the best vehicle for nourishing the extraordinary untapped capacities of all our children. The question is not, Is it possible to educate all children well? but rather, Do we want to do it badly enough?" (p. 4).

After reading, discussing, and reflecting as I worked in my own classroom, I set out once again to implement what I had learned. I began by asking each class to do research papers on a social issue. No one volunteered an issue s/he thought important, so we began watching

Channel One News each day. I introduced the first broadcast by stating our purpose for watching, to become aware of issues facing society today (I also made it clear that I had strong reservations about showing students advertisements). Some of the students could state the topic of the story, but not the larger issue. I began to feel that I was on the wrong track, that this was too hard for them, that such work was inappropriate. Then I remembered Paulo Freire's basic premise that learning should come from the world of the student. The next day we composed a questionnaire to poll our friends and families in an attempt to discover issues that those in our own communities considered important. The students were excited when they compared information with one another. This enthusiasm was markedly different from the dry response to the Channel One activity.

Each student recorded the information from his or her questionnaire on chart paper. One group chose teenage pregnancy; the boys studied the boys' roles in this problem, and the girls studied the who, what, when, where, and why of the girls involved. Both examined prevention programs. The second group chose violence in society, with small-group subtopics of domestic violence, violence on television, and violence in schools.

In this, my fourth, but not final, cycle of democratizing my teaching, I was guided by Glickman's hallmarks of instruction with the democratic purposes of public education (1996, p. 30), including active involvement, escalating degrees of both choice and responsibility, demonstrations of learning in the school and community, and collaboration. I posted these hallmarks around my room to guide our inquiry. We were more successful at some than others; for example, I really hoped students would plan some kind of action that would impact the community, but they did not. However, we became much more of a community ourselves. Students all but stopped the annoying "dissing" of each other. Some who never participated or expressed opinions began doing so. When the nondominant class members spoke, the leaders didn't roll their eyes and otherwise intimidate. They became more respectful of one another. They had important work to do as participants in a democracy.

REFERENCES

Barber, B. (1992). *An aristocracy of everyone: The politics of education and the future of America.* New York: Oxford University Press.

Dayton, J. (1995). Democracy, public schools, and the politics of education. *Review Journal of Philosophy and Social Science, 20,* 135–156.

Delpit, L. (1994). *Other people's children: White teachers, students of color, and other cultural conflicts.* New York: New Press.

Edelsky, C. (1994). Education for democracy. *Language Arts, 71,* 252–257.

Glickman, C. (1996). *Revitalizing the "public" in public universities and colleges: The reciprocal challenge.* Unpublished manuscript.

hooks, b. (1994). *Teaching to transgress: Education as the practice of freedom.* New York: Routledge.

Jefferson, T. (1984). *Writings.* New York: Library of America.

Ladson-Billings, G. (1994). *The dreamkeepers: Successful teachers of African American children.* San Francisco: Jossey-Bass.

Lovitt, T., Cushing, S., & Stump, C. (1994). High school students rate their IEPs: Low opinions and lack of ownership. *Intervention in School and Clinic, 30,* 34–37.

Meier, D. (1995). *The power of their ideas: Lessons for America from a small school in Harlem.* Boston: Beacon Press.

Peters, M. (1990). Someone's missing: The student as an overlooked partner in the IEP process. *Preventing School Failure, 34,* 32–36.

Peterson, M. D. (1994). Jefferson and religious freedom. *The Atlantic Monthly, 274*(6), 113–124.

Ringgold, F. (1992). *Aunt Harriet's underground railroad in the sky.* New York: Crown Publishing.

Shannon, P. (1993). Developing democratic voices. *The Reading Teacher, 47,* 86–94.

Shor, I., & Freire, P. (1987). *A pedagogy for liberation.* New York: Bergin & Garvey.

Turner, A. (1987). *Nettie's trip south.* New York: Simon & Schuster.

CHAPTER 10

Class Actions/School Actions: Widening the Circles of Change

JoBeth Allen, Karen Hankins, Sarah Johnson, Barbara Michalove, and Tricia Taylor

WHAT DIFFERENCE CAN ONE TEACHER, one inquiry project, one novel, one year in a democratic classroom make? Will Tricia's students pause to think the next time they hear someone derided for being gay? Will Jane's students practice democratic pedagogy? Will Suzanne's students be more informed and active citizens as adults? Teachers seldom see the fruits of their nurturing, and we may never know if or how the hundreds of students represented across these chapters have been affected.

THE POWER OF MULTIPLE CONTEXTS IN EDUCATING FOR DEMOCRACY

Reflecting on that critical question—what difference does one experience make—leads to a theoretical crossroads. The belief that one teacher cannot have any effect leads to cynicism, the road to hopelessness, and inaction. Readers who have gotten to this point in the book have probably already rejected that conclusion. Another pathway is faith in the power of one teacher. Readers traveling this path may connect the chapters in this book with the findings of Don Graves and other writing educators, who point out that many professional writers had only one teacher who inspired them to become writers. While this individual inspiration is rewarding when it occurs, becoming a writer and becoming an active citizen in a democracy committed to social justice are different processes. We propose a different path, the power of multiple contexts, or *intercontextuality*. This path offers new vistas of democracy, but reminds us that we have miles to go before we sleep.

Intercontextuality

Intercontextuality builds on the concept of inter*text*uality, the linking of different texts in ways that increase understanding and begin to build a system of beliefs:

> Whenever people engage in a language event, whether it is a conversation, a reading of a book, diary writing, etc., they are engaging in intertextuality. . . . In classrooms, teachers and students are continuously constructing inter-textual relationships . . . [which] can be viewed as constructing a cultural ideology, a system for assigning meaning and significance to what is said and done. (Bloome & Bailey, 1992, pp. 1–2)

This book provides diverse examples of single-classroom contexts. Readers learned how elementary, middle school, and college teachers used multiple texts to create an intertextuality of ideas related to some aspect of democracy. Ana Floriani has extended the concept of intertextuality. She wrote that "contexts, themselves, can be juxtaposed and interactionally invoked by members" (1993, p. 257). When students have the opportunity to juxtapose texts—class discussions, books, their own writing—across contexts, they create *intercontextuality*.

The contexts may be within school (e.g., different classrooms, different years, different classmates and teachers) or across school, home, church, club, or community settings. "These prior contexts, with their socially negotiated roles and relationships and texts and meanings, become resources for members to reexamine past events, to resolve differences in interpretation and understanding, and to lay the foundation for revising and modifying the present," according to Floriani (1993, p. 257). In other words, if students encounter democratic principles and practices across contexts, they multiply meaning potential (Lemke, 1992) and are more likely to apply what they've experienced in new situations.

In an excellent two-year study of a bilingual 5th-grade classroom where the teacher provided multiple opportunities for learning social justice, researcher Louise Jennings (1996) applied Floriani's concept of intercontextuality. Jennings documented ways in which "intertextuality and intercontextuality shape opportunities for learning by multiplying meaning potential (Lemke, 1992) and action potential" (p. 48). She also explored the relationship between how the classroom operated (democratically) and what the students studied (e.g., a five-month "tolerance cycle" that included multiple perspectives on the Jewish Holocaust and on Japanese internment camps in the U.S.). Jennings's premise was that "with congruence between content and practices, students will not only have opportunities to enrich their understanding of what social justice *means*, they will also have opportunities to 'try on' those meanings by *acting* on them" (p. 49).

Jennings found that the teacher created intercontextuality through multiple settings, print resources, and discussions, and by revisiting issues and themes over time. As a result, students developed a repertoire of "resources for democratic learning" (Jennings, 1996, p. 340). Jennings found evidence of these expanded repertoires in the students' language, understandings, and actions. She concluded:

> [S]tudents were provided opportunities to build relationships of meanings, particularly meanings of intolerant and responsible actions, thereby multiplying the potential meanings . . . In addition, these processes provided opportunities for expanding action potential each time students used their expanding understandings and language about responsible actions . . . Moreover, each student also had the opportunity to think about and act on others' meanings and the common knowledge of the class. (p. 345)

Of course, intercontextuality also works in building harmful belief systems, including stereotypes and prejudices. Without examining our assumptions, discussion, and education to the contrary, we fall too easily into thinking of "other people's children" (Delpit, 1994) not only as different, but as deficient. The multiple contexts may include our lack of training and subsequent frustration in trying to teach students who are just learning English; conversations with some of their parents, whom we mistakenly interpret as uninvolved with their children's education; and a headline in the paper about our school's dropping test scores coupled with an editorial about the "threat" of the growing immigrant population. If we aren't vigilant in examining each of these events, we will begin to see "those children" only in terms of problems. We will miss their strengths, their gifts, their potential.

Intercontextuality may happen by chance or by design. Education for democracy is too critical to the future of our society to be left to chance. After a brief examination of schools that are designed for democratic education, we look at what is probably the more common scenario: the potential for one teacher's democratic practices to influence a whole school.

Schoolwide Efforts

Walt Whitman (1871/1967) wrote, "I say that democracy can never prove itself beyond eavil [sic], until it founds and luxuriantly grows its own forms of art, poems, schools, theology, displacing all that exists, or that has been produced anywhere in the past, under opposite influences" (p. 139). There are a few visionary educators who have "grown their own" schools for democratic education. Examples that have been written about (Apple & Beane, 1995) include Central Park East Secondary School (East Harlem), Rindge School of Technical Arts (Cambridge, Massachusetts), Marquette Middle School (Madison, Wisconsin), and La Escuela Fratney (Milwaukee, Wisconsin). We report on other democratic schools in this section, including one where a LEADS member now teaches.

One effort in democratic schooling is Harmony School, an independent elementary school founded in 1977 in Bloomington, Indiana. It was created "to foster the skills necessary for active and constructive participation in our country's democratic process" (Goodman, 1992, p. 52). There is a commitment to involving students in decisions about their school lives. Through Peer Group, Program, and Family Meetings, students and teachers struggle to "understand the relationship between freedom, the exercise of power, and social responsibility" (p. 108). In addition to the democratic processes of establishing their own rights, rules, and responsibilities, students study "issues of race, gender, and social justice" (p. 148).

Lois Holzman (1997) describes other "radical alternatives" to schooling: Sudbury Valley School (SVS) and the Barbara Taylor School (BTS). Both are dedicated to democratic principles, but differ in how democracy is defined and enacted. At SVS, founded in 1968, decisions are made in a democratic process by adults (including parents) and children in a New England town meeting fashion. The school is founded on nurturing individual rights of students; there are no grades, curriculum, or classes. Another model of democratic schooling is the Barbara Taylor School, founded in 1985:

> The radically democratic nature of the Barbara Taylor School goes beyond the participatory, parliamentary structure of the Sudbury Valley School. . . .

> We [BTS] struggle to practice democracy as developmental activity. To us, radical democracy refers to the collective activity of people governing and transforming themselves. The Barbara Taylor School is democratic to the extent that creating the school is inclusionary and voluntary; not to the extent that rules institutionalizing democratic process are followed. (p. 116)

We asked at the beginning of this chapter what difference one teacher, one classroom, one experience might make to students. A related question is what difference a whole school like Harmony or the Barbara Taylor School might make. Cyrene Wells (1996) explored that question when she followed one group of students from a middle school where they had a voice in their education to a high school in which they were relatively powerless. Meadowbrook Community (Middle) School, guided by an evolving, dynamic Vision Statement, held annual Town Meetings of students, teachers, and community members. The community shaped decisions about teaching and learning. At Whitmore High School, there was no vision statement, only a 68-page student handbook of procedures, rules, and consequences. Wells's ethnography documents the disturbing effects this transition had on how students, especially those who struggled in school, viewed themselves as literate people, and how they functioned in both democratic and autocratic settings.

Tricia (Chapter 3) was looking for a school like Meadowbrook Community School or the Barbara Taylor School. She moved to New York City and found a job teaching at a small alternative public high school, the EBC High School for Public Service/Bushwick. The school is in one of the most crime-ridden neighborhoods in Brooklyn. Tricia and other faculty feel they can best address social justice through social action; all students participate in service-learning projects and take courses on community service.

Tricia teaches a writing course called Community Studies. Part of the course focuses on different forms of oppression, such as racism, sexism, anti-Semitism, and heterosexism. Because her students are mostly Latino and African American and live in a low-income community, they know more about oppression than she does. However, she asks her students to think also about how they are privileged. Most discover they are privileged as Christians, Americans-by-birth, and heterosexuals. Although many of the students are openly homophobic, others are not. During discussions of heterosexism, some students openly defend homosexuals. One student trusted Tricia enough to tell her that he is gay. Tricia reflected, "I have taken the role as questioner, yet it is obvious to the students how I must view heterosexism because I include it as a form of oppression. As I learned from my experiences during student teaching, it is important for me to be consistent, not to choose one form of oppression as more harmful than another."

Tricia found a school with a philosophy and a curriculum that promote education for social justice. Mollie and Suzanne are in doctoral programs at the University of Pennsylvania and the University of Georgia (respectively), where they are studying education for democracy full-time. Eury, Jane, and JoBeth continue to seek ways to democratize their teacher education classes. Barbara, Sarah, and Karen have stayed in their schools, but their work is having an impact beyond their classrooms, as we illustrate in the final section.

WIDENING CIRCLES, FROM CLASSROOMS TO SCHOOLS

We conclude *Class Actions* with a partial answer to the question, What difference can one teacher make? In a legal class action, one group of people acts on behalf of a larger group of people with similar claims. If the class action is successful, the whole group benefits. When members of the LEADS group acted within our own classrooms, we were starting with the people and places we knew best and those we were most responsible for, ourselves and our students. The kind of systemic change Edelsky challenged us to enact seemed overwhelming. But we are beginning to see that our *classroom actions* may become *class actions* when we are willing to take the next step, to widen the circle by sharing insights and issues with others in our schools.

Barbara's Classroom/Barbara's School

The cultural clashes Barbara (Chapter 2) observed in her classroom were taking place throughout her school, especially in relation to the recently immigrated Hispanic students. The children rarely talked to their classroom teachers, but they did talk—in Spanish—with their ESOL (English for Speakers of Other Languages) teacher, Maria Zavala-Waterman. They did not feel welcome in the school. They felt the tension of being outsiders in two established communities, neighborhood, and school. They complained that classmates picked on them. "My teacher hates me—she yells at me," they added. These differences in interaction and in expectation may have been cultural. Maria noticed other cultural gulfs. At a conference between a Spanish-speaking father and a young English-speaking teacher, Maria translated. Afterwards, the teacher was furious. "He never even looked at me the whole time. He never said a word to me!" she fumed. Maria explained, "In his culture, it would have been rude for him to look directly at you. That's true of the children, too. If they looked straight at an adult who was talking to them, they would be scolded for being rude."

Maria talked with Barbara, who had observed similar problems. They brought the issue up among teachers, who recognized the need to find better ways of meeting the needs of this new population. They formed a multiracial committee. Barbara invited a consultant from a nonprofit organization in Atlanta, Bridging the Gap, to speak with the committee. This group has worked mostly with police forces but is starting to get lots of calls from schools, although Barbara's school will be the first one they will work with. The consultant's focus is on bridging the gaps that may occur between cultures because of different norms, experiences, educational background, styles of communicating, and body language.

The consultant suggested an outside assessment of the specific needs of the school, stressing that no canned series of workshops would be effective. She will work with faculty and with students, and she will help faculty talk with students, parents, and each other to get a better understanding of the situation. She warned that "sometimes things get worse before they can get better," but assured them that she wouldn't just stir things up and then walk away. The assumptions, stereotypes, misunderstandings, and fears have solidified over time and multiple contexts, creating the current cultural gaps. Building new understandings—bridging the gaps—will take time and multiple contexts as well.

Sarah's Classroom/Sarah's School

Class actions broaden and intercontextual links are created when two teachers begin to talk about educating for a democratic society. Just as Barbara and Maria began the change process at their school, Sarah Johnson (Chapter 9) found colleagues for change in her middle school. After attending a conference recently of Annenberg Rural Challenge schools, Sarah and a colleague pondered the keynote speaker's question: What is your school doing to break the cycle of poverty? They brought that question back to the school. After being told by the Board of Education that they needed to "create a level playing field for our students by raising standardized test scores," teachers questioned that simplistic approach. They asked broader questions about providing equal opportunities. For example, there are excellent after-school activities, but only the students whose parents can pick them up participate, and those are by and large more affluent families. The rural poor must ride the buses that leave when the bell rings. Will the school community address these systemic inequities?

They will try. The dialogue has already begun, and teachers have implemented one schoolwide action to make the school a place where everyone feels accepted. Sarah's colleague, Penny Ogren, was disturbed by the fighting among students. She had been a peer mediator in her own student days. Penny led an effort to teach children more positive, less violent ways of handling conflict through literature discussions. Teachers selected one novel at each grade level that all students would read, and planned activities using resources such as *Creating the Peaceable School* (Bodine, Crawford, & Schrumf, 1994) and *Conflict Resolution in the Middle School* (Kreidler, 1994) that helped students analyze causes for and responses to conflicts. They applied these as they read *Maniac Magee* (Spinelli, 1990) in 6th grade, *Leroy and the Old Man* (Butterworth, 1989) in 7th grade, and *Scorpions* (Myers, 1988) in 8th grade. The response from the students has been overwhelmingly positive. Fighting, bullying, racial tension, "in groups," and the quest for harmony and acceptance are issues that reach to the core of democratic schooling.

These examples of intercontextuality provide multiple entryways. Barbara talked with a like-minded colleague, and they took the issue to the whole faculty, who decided to contact a resource with expertise in a very different context—community police work. Sarah read widely from educators who worked toward democracy across times and places. She also talked with colleagues. One of those was Penny, who drew on her experience as a student. Penny's teachers had created a context for democratic schooling that benefited another school decades later. Sometimes we create intercontextuality intentionally; sometimes it is serendipitous. Always, it must be an intentional goal, even when the impact is not obvious or immediate.

There are many issues that affect how teachers individually and collectively work to democratize education. How can we sustain these efforts when more and more curriculum is being imposed? How can we convince administrators and the public that social justice issues in the curriculum are valid and vital content, that they are not "taking away from" the basics but *are* the basics? With the beliefs of many on the Christian Right that adults should break children's wills, control their thinking, and make them obedient to authority (Berliner, 1997), how can teachers promote constructivist learning and democratic decision-making? With ever-increasing pressure for standardized test performance, how do we help students develop as readers, artists, mathematicians, and scientists *within* democratic structures and *through* democratic curricula?

These are questions we ask ourselves daily in our classrooms, and monthly when we dialogue in LEADS meetings. What can we do beyond our classrooms? What can we do together that we might not be able to do individually? Should we be writing letters to the editor, attending school board meetings, lobbying legislators? Sarah is drawing on years of environmental activism strategies to move us in this direction next year. We are inspired by teachers who have joined forces to effect change, like the literacy teachers in Madison, Wisconsin, who organized, wrote, spoke, and became effective political agents to save their Reading Recovery program from budget cuts (Keresty, O'Leary, & Wortley, 1998). We are challenged by groups of educators like the faculty at the University of Massachusetts at Amherst School of Education who over the last 20 years have developed a strong theoretical foundation and pedagogical framework for teaching for social justice both in single-issue and multiple-issue college courses (Adams, Bell, & Griffin, 1997).

We hope this book is useful to other literacy educators who, like us, live these questions and challenges. We offer examples of students reading multiple texts, accessing a wide range of resources, building vocabularies, writing in multiple genres, and using language and literacy as integral tools for understanding difficult concepts. Students in these classrooms are actively engaged in learning.

In this final chapter, we've presented illustrative stories of talk that has gone beyond our ongoing LEADS discussions and our individual classrooms to foster whole-school dialogues and in some cases whole-school change. The last story is Karen's.

Karen's Classroom/Karen's School

In one local school district, parents can choose where their children go to school, so schools are encouraged to have an identity. The district administrators require that Title 1 schools submit a schoolwide, research-based plan for the teaching of reading. The expectation was that the plan would be the name of a reading program such as Success for All. Karen Hankins's school has many highly experienced teachers who have resisted this one-program-fits-all mentality. Many teachers would identify themselves as whole language teachers, but for political reasons, they don't use this term for the school. In the past they have explained that they followed a "modified New Zealand literature-based approach," and that their identity is as "a reading school—everyone here loves to read."

The problem is that not everyone there does read. The school population shifted after school choice, and is now upper-middle-class suburban and poor urban, with school success, including reading, highly correlated to these two socioeconomic status indicators. Teachers who saw their "good school" and "reading school" reputation changing and their test scores dropping began to blame the urban children, almost all of whom are African American. They knew their instruction was successful with the suburban children, some African American, some international, most European American. So they began to think of the new children as "those children," and to say, "Those children just can't learn, or don't want to learn, or their parents just aren't interested."

It was at this juncture of district expectation and their own frustration with the way the school was changing that the "reading focus group" began reading the research literature. The group selected over 30 articles and chapters on the teaching of reading by authors such as Anne Dyson, Marie Clay, Steve Stahl, and Lucy Calkins, and from the extensive literature on Reading Recovery. Karen contributed specific information about the teaching of African American children and children of poverty by Lisa Delpit, Michelle Foster, and others.

The group met weekly for several months to write goals, objectives to meet the goals, and strategies to meet the objectives. After one meeting, someone scrawled an anonymous note across the minutes: "Remember, let's not set too lofty a goal, considering our population." Throughout the discussions, Karen urged the group to truly "consider our population." She shared insights she was developing (Chapter 5) that what we say, how we listen, and what we do are just as important as any instructional methods. The discussions were very painful. Some of the teachers, both African American and European American, were openly hostile, accusing Karen of saying they weren't working hard enough. She argued that they all—herself included—didn't need to work harder, but differently. She explained how much more effective her teaching was when she listened to children read aloud, analyzed running records of their reading, and provided instruction geared to each child's needs. Teachers argued that there wasn't enough time, that they didn't have aides to help them, that "some kids reach a cutoff point and just can't learn any more."

Karen replied, "The day I believe there are children in my class who just can't learn is they day I leave teaching."

The group dispersed, angry, tense, unsure of how to proceed. But the next day, in confidence, someone told Karen and like-minded colleague Kay Stahl, "Thank you. It had to be said." The group convinced them to write the rationale for their plan and pulled together to tell her what to write. "Start with 'We believe all children can learn,'" one teacher said as the others nodded. "Write that with lines under it." In order to reach each child, they decided to blend strategies they had read about on assessment, such as running records and benchmark texts, with their expertise in teaching literacy strategies within a literature-based program. They would learn new ways of understanding what children bring to school and how they are learning, and they would build their instruction on these new understandings.

The group chose Karen to present their rationale and plan to the full faculty and central office personnel. She began with a story about her father, one of "those mill kids" integrated with the "city kids" in a scene reminiscent of Heath's (1983) study of low-income mill workers and their middle-income classmates. He couldn't read, or spell, and felt stupid and outcast, until his 4th grade teacher talked about his strengths and showed him respect in front of the class during a geography lesson. He went on to become a geography teacher, and later to earn a doctoral degree.

The parallel to the recent urban/suburban integration at their school was evident. "Those kids" can learn. Next Karen quoted Maxine Green's (1985) observation that one of the marks of a master teacher is the ability to "shape and reshape the materials of their craft" and Lisa Delpit's maxim that "we do not see with our eyes or hear with our ears but with our beliefs" (1994, p. 46). Then she asked the faculty and administrators to examine their beliefs as she presented the following statement from the reading focus group:

1. We believe reading is central to all learning.
2. We believe it is our job to teach EVERY child to read.
3. We believe ALL children can succeed at high academic levels when provided with opportunities that match their learning styles and developmental stages.
4. We believe teachers are learners. We will learn *about* our students by participating in staff development that focuses on the latest classroom research; we will learn *from* our students by implementing multiple assessment instruments with the intent of matching instructional strategies to student needs.
5. We believe the amount of time spent reading is positively correlated with reading success. We will provide increased opportunities to read during the school day and will try to involve parents and the community in enlarging "reading after hours" time.

The room was silent for a moment. Some teachers had tears in their eyes. Through the pain of having to confront their failures, Karen and her dedicated, experienced colleagues began the slow process of systemic change. They began by looking at themselves and their assumptions, laid open for scrutiny by honest dialogue. They committed themselves to looking at, and listening to, their children with different eyes and ears. Others in the school thanked the group "for recognizing the strengths that this faculty has, and our commitment to educating all children." Karen, who had agonized through the process, fearing at times that her views were tearing the faculty apart, said, "It was the first time I felt like

I had a place in the school since I came back from graduate school. Through my studies I transformed the way I see and think and feel, the way I teach. I knew I had to use what I've had the privilege to study to influence others."

There are parallels with Barbara's process of "circling in," starting outside in order to look inward. Karen and her colleagues started with the literature, and were eventually able to apply it to themselves, because one person had taken the risk to say, "The children aren't the problem. I'm the problem." This self-knowledge is both sobering and exhilarating. To recognize ourselves as part of the problem revels our power to make a difference, our power to influence the lives of the children we teach. It is up to us to choose the path wisely, to accept the challenge to educate our students and ourselves for democracy.

REFERENCES

Adams, M., Bell, L., & Griffin, P. (1997). *Teaching for diversity and social justice.* New York: Routledge.

Apple, M., & Beane, J. (1995). *Democratic schools.* Alexandria, VA: Association for Supervision and Curriculum Development.

Berliner, D. (1997). Educational psychology meets the Christian Right: Differing views of children, schooling, teaching, and learning. *Teachers College Record, 98*(3), 381–416.

Bloome, D., & Bailey, F. (1992). From linguistics and education, a direction for research on language and literacy. In R. Beach, J. Green, M. Kamil, & T. Shanahan (Eds.), *Multiple disciplinary perspectives on language and literacy research* (pp. 181–210). Urbana, IL: National Conference on Research in English and National Council of Teachers of English.

Bodine, R., Crawford, D., & Schrumf, F. (1994). *Creating the peaceable school: A comprehensive program for teaching conflict resolution.* Champaign, IL: Research Press.

Butterworth, W. E. (1989). *Leroy and the old man.* New York: Scholastic.

Delpit, L. (1994). *Other people's children: White teachers, students of color, and other cultural conflicts.* New York: New Press.

Floriani, A. (1993). Negotiating what counts: Roles and relationships, texts and contexts, content and meaning. *Linguistics and Education, 5,* 241–274.

Goodman, J. (1992). *Elementary schooling for critical democracy.* Albany, NY: State University of New York Press.

Green, M. (1985). A philosophical look at merit and mastery in teaching. *Elementary School Journal, 86,* 17–26.

Heath, S. (1983). *Ways with words.* Cambridge, UK: Cambridge University Press.

Holzman, L. (1997). *Schools for growth: Radical alternatives to current educational models.* Mahwah, NJ: Erlbaum.

Jennings, L. (1996). *Multiple contexts for learning social justice: An ethnographic and sociolinguistic study of a fifth grade bilingual class.* Unpublished doctoral dissertation, University of California at Santa Barbara, Santa Barbara, CA.

Keresty, B., O'Leary, S., & Wortley, D. (1998). *You can make a difference: A teacher's guide to political action.* Portsmouth, NH: Heinemann.

Kreidler, W. J. (1994). *Conflict resolution in the middle school: A curriculum teaching guide.* Cambridge, MA: Educators for Social Responsibility.

Lemke, J. (1992). Intertextuality and educational research. *Linguistics and Education, 4,* 257–267.

Myers, W. D. (1988). *Scorpions.* New York: Harper & Row.

Spinelli, J. (1990). *Maniac Magee.* Boston, MA: Little, Brown.

Wells, C. (1996). *Literacies lost: When students move from a progressive middle school to a traditional high school.* New York: Teachers College Press.

Whitman, W. (1871/1967). Democratic vistas. In S. Bradley, R. Beatty, & E. Long (Eds.), *The American tradition in literature,* volume 2 (3rd ed.) (pp. 139–150). New York: Norton.

Education for Democracy

Carole Edelsky

WITH A TITLE LIKE "Education for Democracy"—with those two big words in it, *education* and *democracy*—the word I want to hold up to the light first is *for*. It could mean education *for* use by an existing, living, breathing democracy. It could also mean education *for* bringing about a democracy—because we surely don't have one now. That's the *for* I mean. Despite secret ballots and slogans like "majority rules," we don't have a democracy. Some of us think we do. Lots of us wish we did. We've got some of the rhetoric and even some of the governmental structures. But we're a long way from living in a democracy.

A democracy is a system, as Pat Shannon (1993) says, in which people participate meaningfully in decisions that affect their lives. To quote John Cabral (personal communication, 1993), a progressive city planner in Chicago, it is a system where people consciously and rationally decide together *how* and *what* to produce and consume; or to quote Peter Johnston (1992), it is a system where there is genuine negotiation of societal goals and meanings. Each definition emphasizes participation. But it's participation among equals, negotiation among equals, not participation where a few are more equal than the rest. Each definition also emphasizes *significant* participation, not just having a vote on options already determined behind the scenes—in essence, eliminating official "behind-the-scene-ness."

In a democracy, there wouldn't be the kind of situation in the United States that Shannon (1993) described in an article called "Developing Democratic Voices"—a situation of increasing poverty for the many and

Reprinted with permission from the National Council of Teachers of English. This article originally appeared in the April 1994 issue (Vol. 71) of *Language Arts*.

increasing wealth for the few, a situation that didn't just happen but is the result of deliberate government tax policy.

William Greider wrote a book called *Who Will Tell the People?* (1992). He too talks about government tax policy and how it makes the rich richer and the poor poorer. Like Shannon, he goes on to reveal just how that tax policy came about. No surprise—it happened as a result of behind-the-scenes activity of lobbyists paid for by the rich. Greider provides the names, meetings, quoted sources, dates, and numbers behind this tax policy and behind many of the other ongoing scandals in our mock democracy where significant participation is only for the few. One scandalous example is the savings and loan debacle, with profits going into private pockets and losses now coming out of public pockets—in other words, with privatized profits and socialized losses. Or there's the case of laws for increasing workplace safety (which people who work at all kinds of jobs, including jobs in education, continue to demand). Those laws are being subverted by big companies able to afford lengthy litigation and then later to negotiate down the fines. (It's cheaper to be fined than to clean up the place.) Or despite the fact that the majority of people in this country express strong values in favor of cleaning up the environment, one environmental protection effort after the other fails. Corporations have applied undue pressure when exact wordings of regulations were being written and definitions of such things as "ample margins of safety" were being determined, and the White House and the Office of Management and Budget have engaged in giant "ticket fixing" for corporations that got caught. Or there's the example of the 20 years' worth of corporate resistance to laws for improving the safety of automobiles despite the expressed desires of the majority for safer cars. And on and on with the scandals.

In a system where wealth buys the right to overrule majority wishes, where wealth buys the power to make decisions that affect the life and livelihood of everybody else, you can't have a democracy. In a system where corporations are so privileged that they can write the laws as well as decide which laws they'll obey, you can't have a democracy. A few can unduly influence decisions in which, if it were a democracy, everybody is supposed to have an equal say. That's why Shannon's article on democratic voices begins with *economics*, with statistics on the poverty of many in America and the wealth of a few, and with one example from recent history (the example of tax policy) of how these two conditions—wealth and poverty—depend on each other. That's why Greider lays the blame for the betrayal of American democratic *political* processes at the feet of "organized money." And that's why what may be "good for business"— for example, the media mergers that replaced hundreds of separately owned newspapers, radio and TV stations, film companies, and book publishers with just 20 multimedia conglomerates—is noted by critics as "bad for democracy."

Now it's not that every individual who has a business can make everybody else do what's good for their business. And it's not that all rich individuals conspire to overpower all individuals who have less. It's that a *system* exists for promoting the power of the wealthy. Just as a system exists for giving more privilege to what's best for corporations. Just as a system exists that gives greater power and privilege to "whiteness" (even if an individual white person is the secretary and the black person is the superintendent). (What I mean by privilege here is what Peggy McIntosh [1988] described. It is unearned benefits like being able to take for granted that the color of my skin won't make me seem less reliable if I want to cash a check some place or being able to assume that if a traffic cop pulls me over, it won't be because of my race.) It's an existing system that gives whiteness that privilege, just as another existing system gives dominance to maleness (even if, in a specific case, she is *his* boss). In other words, we can't have a democracy—a system in which people participate meaningfully and without system-derived privilege or prejudice in decisions that affect their lives—when we have systems of domination.

Politics is about who gets what, where, and how—who gets money, who gets jobs, who gets diplomas, who gets good health care, who gets high-quality literature in classrooms, who gets turns at talk, who gets listened to, who gets valued socially (because resources aren't just material—they're also social; and politics isn't just about what's public—it's also about what's personal). Democracy is *one* way to decide who gets what. It's one *political* approach to *economy*, to the allocation of societal resources. Undue influence, from a grossly uneven allocation of resources, prohibits democracy because those who have already "gotten" set things up so that they'll keep on getting. That is, there's undue influence over who gets to have undue influence. Now I'm not saying that if you want a democracy, you want everybody to have an equal chance to have undue influence. Instead, you want to get undue influence—systematic domination—out of the picture altogether.

Education for bringing about democracy would aim at helping put an end to the systems of domination that create the condition we have now—a condition of decidedly unequal influence over who gets what. The last thing we need, therefore, in creating education for bringing about democracy is to do something that further entrenches some system of domination. Bringing corporate dominance right inside the door of education by being partners with business (or using business-inspired materials or business-made TV shows like Channel One) or by adopting business ways as models is an example of such entrenchment. Corporations like to tout the contributions they make to schools, but they don't talk about how many state and local tax dollars they cheat schools out of by demanding property tax breaks in exchange for locating in an area. General Motors, for example, brags about being a friend to education through giving gifts; but it got Tarrytown, New York, to cut GM's taxes by $1,000,000 each year, which forced the town to lay off teachers and postpone school repairs. Some friend of education! Moreover, as Alex Molnar asks rhetorically in an article in *Rethinking Schools* (1992), should students (and teachers) learn about accountability from CEOs who double their own salaries while laying off thousands of workers? Or should they learn about good citizenship and social responsibility from the Wall Street sharpies and S and L con artists who have gone a long way toward ruining our economy with their financial manipulations? Or should we teach about nutrition with dittos from Chef Boyardee or about nuclear power with materials from the electric power industry? And when we think business has changed its ways—that corporations no longer operate with the factor model that schools borrowed from them years ago; that they now are humanized through TQM (total quality management), decentralized decision making, and techniques for consensus building; and that schools should, therefore, once again look to business as a model for schooling—we should look again. The new corporate model referred to as liberation management, in a best seller by that name (see Kauffman, 1993), ironically was borrowed from 1960s anti-business activists. And not surprisingly, it has been adapted to business needs in a way that fits—what else?—business needs. That is, the essence of these ideas has been turned inside out. So a CEO in Milwaukee talks about participatory decision making for workers but busts their union. To cite a review of *Liberation Management,* by L. A. Kauffman (1993), promoting empowered management means getting managers to be self-actualizing, not getting managers to seize power. The term "revolutionary" gets coopted to mean revolutionary new detergent. Radical decentralization becomes a way to justify firing full-time employees and bring in contractors who hire part-timers who don't get benefits.

Bringing business into education is hardly the way to educate *for* democracy, for putting an end to systems of domination—including corporate domination—that prevent us from having a democracy. Instead, the first step is to *see* those systems of domination, to become aware, to see how *systemic* (not idiosyncratic) privilege linked to a system driven by profit prevents us from participating equally and meaningfully—that is, from having a democracy.

We come to that awareness, in all its detail, by getting critical, by taking what is taken for granted (like having principals for schools or like selling medicine for profit), and by taking what is seen as business as usual (such as letting a test score keep people out or letting the guys think the idea was theirs) and examining it, figuring out where it came from, what it's connected to, whose interest it serves.

I realize that it's difficult to get critical in the United States in general and in schools in particular. When the musical refrain "Don't worry, be happy" is so commonly appreciated that it becomes a bumper sticker or a T-shirt, it's hard to whip up widespread enthusiasm for exposing trouble or, worse, for making the effort to understand the sources of trouble. When you add educators' desires to please and be liked, and the significant pressures to avoid controversy, critique becomes even more difficult. Nevertheless, critique remains the first step in a three-part undertaking in educating *for* (bringing about) democracy. The other two parts are: (1) hope—something that comes from learning about prior struggles against systems of domination, struggles that *did* have some effect; and (2) action— linking students and ourselves to others who are doing something, no matter how small, to end systems of domination. Those systems—of class, race, gender, whose impact is heightened by their relation to profit and the bottom line—seep into all aspects of life: public and private, in school and out. Growing up within them, we've breathed them in so they're part of our thinking, our values, and our opinions. In other words, we'd have no trouble finding things to examine that would lead to exposing some system of domination. Those systems show up everywhere, if we just look. They're also extremely resistant to dismantling. So we can't expect to get rid of them easily. Still, we can take heart from stories of early labor struggles, civil rights actions, and women's rights efforts. If enough people work at it with commitment, those systems of domination could finally collapse.

What might this mean, very specifically, for language education? If critique were to be one of our main activities, and bringing down the barriers to democracy were to be a serious goal, we would have to re-theorize language education. That's because most of our current progressive theories and practices—such as reader response theory; sociopsycholinguistic models of reading; transactional theory in reading; literacies as social practices, curriculum as inquiry; whole language practices; writing process practices; whole language as described theoretically by me, among others; and so on—can as easily support *avoiding* looking at white privilege, for example, as they support looking *at* it. Those progressive theories and practices are correct, I believe, but they don't go far enough. They don't actively and primarily—*as a first priority*—tie language to power, tie text interpretation to societal structures, or tie reading and writing to perpetuating or resisting.

Critical theorists do those things, but, from my perspective, their theories about processes of written language learning doom their project of critical literacy. They may get kids to be critical, but with their often underlying skills view of reading, for example, they're no more likely than noncritical traditionalists to get kids to be literate. Progressive language educators help kids become literate, but we don't necessarily make them critical. Although progressive language educators' theories-in-practice *do* consider power relationships in text interpretations, for instance, or in curriculum planning, and although we *do* have an implicit opposition to hierarchies woven into our frameworks, we don't take the role of language in perpetuating or constituting systems of domination and make that the central topic, something all the rest is seen in relation to. Progressive language educators' theories-in-practice, therefore, could just as well be a kinder, gentler way to maintain those systems of dominance—a kinder, gentler way of keeping us far from a democracy as ever. To get closer, as I said, I think we have to re-theorize language education.

What I mean by re-theorizing might become clearer if I give an example from feminist theory. For two decades, feminist theory has argued for the personal as being political, for the theoretical truth of individual women's stories, for disavowing some patriarchal notion of "woman" that affects all women, and for valuing the plurality of women. However, as Carmen Luke (1992) argues, that theory, along with other postmodern, poststructural theories, paints women into a theoretical corner. If ultimately, we're so plural, so individually different, then we have no grounds to claim anything about women's issues. The "we" has become theoretically unfounded and therefore depoliticized. Luke argues that feminist theory is correct in attending to individual women's voices, correct to refuse to accept some essential patriarchy-defined woman. But still, she urges re-theorizing, thinking through some key epistemological issues, in order to keep the theoretical value of individual women's experience while foregrounding the global, economic, and cultural oppression women share. Otherwise, the theory itself subverts the project of women's emancipation by theoretically denying that there is any validity to a grouping called "women." You can't have class action if there's no class.

I think there's a parallel here with language education. As we stand now, our theories in language education focus on individuals, but our goal (if it's democracy we're after) is societal. We aim for a democracy—a *societal* system dependent on equally weighted participation, on an absence of undue influence. Our theories, however, act as though language expression and language processing, although socially situated and constrained by social conventions, are primarily acts of individuals. Our theories-in-practice fail to take as their central focus the way language learning and language use are tied not only to people's individual experiences but also to people's societal positions, to their structured privilege, to their greater or lesser power, and to the interests of the groups they represent. We can't hope to change what's societal if we keep backgrounding what's societal.

Re-theorizing language education doesn't mean discrediting the idea of reading as a sociopsycholinguistic process. It doesn't mean denying that all language conventions are social practices that change from culture to culture. It doesn't mean throwing out the notion that people use their prior experience to create a text, and therefore, since people don't have identical experiences, the texts and interpretations they create will be different. It doesn't mean eliminating inquiry from language pedagogy.

Re-theorizing language education to make it serve education *for* democracy means highlighting the relationship of language and power. It means trying to understand the connections between the language-power issue and the idea of sociopsycholinguistic process, the idea of literacies as social practices, the idea of reading as transaction, and so on, keeping the language-power issue central. It means figuring out and then spelling out how systems of domination are part of reading and writing, part of classroom interaction, part of texts of all kinds—and doing that as our constant and primary, not secondary, enterprise. It means talking about pedagogies differently. For instance, instead of talking about whole language as a perspective in practice, maybe we'd talk about whole language as a set of commitments in practice (to democracy, for example, or to ending systems of privilege dominance). The perspective would then be framed as what views of reading, for instance, are required if you have such commitments. Instead of talking about accepting children's plausible interpretations of literature and what they write, we'd talk about the positions people are put in by texts, what premises we're positioned to accept, and how we accept or resist those; and we'd do that in part by using kids' interpretations—their writings, their readings of things—as material to explore. Maybe we'd background reading altogether and foreground readings. Or, in both our practice and our theorizing about response to literature, instead of being satisfied with personal responses to literature, with identifying what resonates with self and family, we'd start with those; and then, as Bess Altwerger (person communication, 1993) urges, we'd encourage a sustained look at the social issues that are suggested by so many pieces of literature and that languish unexamined in personal responses. Instead of theorizing about child-centeredness, as though children's interests in dinosaurs, for example, came from them and not from a zillion dollars of Disney's and other companies' ad and product campaigns, we might think about system-centeredness, or what sounds even worse, child-as-being-through-whom-the-culture-speaks-centeredness. We might find some term that helps us to think about the "center" of curriculum as being more complexly derived than a choice between either child-centered or teacher-centered and as being more *necessarily* connected to our democratic goals for ending systems of dominance than process-centered or inquiry-centered.

And all the while, we would be wary of the tendency to domesticate, knowing how easy it is to tone down or distort ideas that challenge the system, such as turning empowerment into a psychological process, or twisting being critical into meaning critical-thinking skills, or taking the term "praxis" and making it Praxis I and Praxis II (the name of components of a software program called Learning Plus put out by ETS, designed to coach students who fail the PPST—the basic skills test used as a gatekeeper for many teacher preparation programs). The system-challenging notion of praxis—with its meanings of recursive reflexivity in the service of political consciousness—action, theory (including political reflection), more action, more political reflection/theory development, and so on— has now been stripped away. Instead, ETS offers us Praxis I, with the now-reduced meaning (to quote ETS) of "meaningful practice" of skills like using correct conjunctions and skimming for the main points.

Re-theorizing will help put critique at the center of language education. But many of us, myself included, need something else. We need help in learning how to critique with students; how to find the systemic corporatism with its bottom-line mentality; how to find sexism, racism, and classism in whatever we're interrogating *without bashing students over the head with it*. That's the hard part. We could look to writings on critical pedagogy by Giroux or McLaren or Simon for help (for example, Giroux, 1983; McLaren, 1986; Simon, 1992). And they *do* help by explicating theory at length. But, for myself, I know that right now I need to be looking to the writings of the handful of public school classroom teachers who make ending privilege and *systemic* domination the center of their teaching. I'm thinking here of Alex McLeod of Great Britain; Avril Aitken, publishing in the *English Quarterly*; Linda Christensen; Bill Bigelow; Bob Peterson; and others who write for *Rethinking Schools*. (And right here, I want to suggest that if you're seriously interested in educating for democracy, you should subscribe to that newspaper: *Rethinking Schools*, 1001 E. Keefe Ave., Milwaukee, WI 53212, $12.50 per year. It's put out by teachers in Milwaukee and is one of the most important, well-written educational periodicals around.)

There are some distinct advantages to seeking out classroom teachers who do it well to guide us in developing our own ways to get critical in language curriculum. First, their writing is theoretical both in the sense of practice always being theoretical and also in the sense of making explicit their theoretical claims about language. Their claims tend to follow the critical sociolinguistics of Norman Fairclough (1989) from Great Britain and Allan Luke (Luke & Walton, 1993) from Australia. Second, their writing is vivid, accessible, and not off-putting. Third, their writing is full of classroom detail. Unlike the writings of educational critical theorists, which are underspecified in the extreme, articles by Christensen, for instance, not only provide theory; but they also provide descriptions of classroom scenes, dialogue, teacher's thinking, and students' work. These writings remind me of what it was like to read Graves 15 years ago. It's not that I needed method; I needed vision. Reading those vivid portraits, *with commentary* about something like writing workshops, which I'd never seen or experienced first hand, helped me—and a few million others—gain the confidence to change both my understanding and my practice.

Now I think it's time to do that again—to get our consciousness raised—this time about those systems of domination and to figure out what to do in classrooms to help stop them. Just as we found communities of colleagues who wanted to study and support each other and change together in relation to studying children's work with Pat Carini, for example, or just as we formed communities to learn more about whole language after we read or heard Ken or Yetta Goodman, or Dorothy Watson, or Jerry Harste in the late 70s, we need to seek out others now. Especially do we need to seek out elementary school teachers like Mary Langan, who asks her 5th graders to look at the social studies materials her Scottsdale, Arizona, school has on Pilgrims and Indians and ask themselves, Who wrote this? Whose idea is this? Do you think this is the way the Indians would tell it? And then Mary Langan, and I, and a few others in our group, and you in the groups you form need to help each other extend the asking of those few questions about the Thanksgiving story on one day into a sustained inquiry of that issue—the issue of whose story is being told here, and who benefits, and how they benefit from *this* version of the story being the one that is told.

Few of us grew up or were prepared for teaching in classrooms that educated FOR democracy, for bringing about an end to systemic privilege and domination, for creating a climate where people can have a significant say in what affects their lives. But few of us grew up or were prepared for teaching in classrooms where kids could write to make sense of their lives or where they could learn to read by connecting to authors. Yet look how far we've come on that road. Learning to educate for democracy—and figuring out how to do it and keep our jobs—is going to be harder. But it's time to start down that road. Maybe we can do it—together.

REFERENCES

Fairclough, N. (1989). *Language and power*. London: Longman.

Giroux, H. (1983). *Theory and resistance in education*. South Hadley, MA: Bergin & Garvey.

Greider, W. (1992). *Who will tell the people?* New York: Simon and Schuster.

Johnston, P. (1992, December). *Assessment as social practice*. Paper presented at the National Reading Conference, San Antonio, TX.

Kauffman, L. A. (1993, May 24). Democracy in the suites. *The Nation*, pp. 712–713.

Luke, A., & Walton, C. (in press). Critical reading. In T. Husen & T. Posthewaite (Eds.), *International encyclopedia of education*. London: Pergamon.

Luke, C. (1992). The politicized "I" and depoliticized "we": The politics of theory in postmodern feminisms. *Social Semiotics, 2*, 1–20.

McIntosh, P. (1988). *White privilege and male privilege: A personal account of coming to see correspondences through work in women's studies* (Working Paper No. 189). Wellesley, MA: Wellesley College, Center for Research on Women.

McLaren, P. (1986). *School as a ritual performance*. London, England: Routledge and Kegan Paul.

Molnar, A. (1992). Fears about business involvement. *Rethinking Schools, 7*, 7.

Shannon, P. (1993). Developing democratic voices. *The Reading Teacher, 47*, 86–94.

Simon, R. (1992). *Teaching against the grain*. New York: Bergin & Garvey.

About the Editor and the Contributors

JoBeth Allen is a professor of Language Education at the University of Georgia. She is a collaborative action researcher, with interest in the intersections of progressive educational practices, literacy teaching and learning, and social justice issues.

Eurydice Bouchereau Bauer is an assistant professor of Reading Education at the University of Georgia. Her research interests are biliteracy development in preschool children, assessment of diverse populations, and the implications of cultural diversity for teaching and learning.

Mollie Blackburn taught middle school language arts and high school English in Los Angeles and Athens, Georgia. She is currently a doctoral student at the University of Pennsylvania in the Reading/Writing/Literacy program of the Language Education Department, where she is pursuing her interest in literacy and social justice issues.

Cathy Crumley teaches fourth grade at Peachtree Elementary in Norcross, Georgia. Cathy and her students are focusing on daily class meetings as a forum for democratic problem-solving.

Julie Dickerson teaches fifth grade at York Elementary in Raleigh, North Carolina. She is also a graduate student at Meredith College. Her teacher research focuses on how democracy in the classroom can empower struggling readers.

Melissa Francis is a special education assistant at Whately Elementary School in Whately, Massachusetts. Melissa is studying techniques for literature discussions and journals to use with her 5th-grade literature group.

Karen Hankins teaches first grade at Whit Davis Elementary School in Athens, Georgia. She is interested in dissecting attitudes of teachers toward students that distance students from the curriculum. For her dissertation, she is examining her own narratives about her students and their narratives, contextualizing them in her reflective journal writing.

Sarah Johnson, a former special education teacher, currently teaches 6th grade language arts in Lexington, Georgia. She is interested in finding ways to involve the broad spectrum of the public who have a stake in public education in the dialogues about schooling in order to broaden the base of voices from the community that shape educational policy.

After teaching middle school for five years in the Clarke County School District in Athens, **Suzanne S. McCotter** is currently working on her Ph.D. in Middle School Education at the University of Georgia. Her dissertation research focuses on the LEADS group during the 1997–1998 school year, and positions the group as one way for teachers and teacher educators to participate in true professional development.

Barbara Michalove currently teaches 1st grade and is the Literacy Coordinator for the Extended Learning Literacy Initiative at Fourth Street Elementary School in Athens, Georgia. She has studied children who struggle in school, and ways of connecting home and school literacy practices with co-researchers Betty Shockley and JoBeth Allen.

Tricia Taylor teaches at a small public high school in Brooklyn, New York. In her writing class called Community Studies, students explore issues of identity, social injustice, and social action through their reading, writing, and activism.

Jane West is an Assistant Professor in the Department of Education at Agnes Scott College in Decatur, Georgia. Her current research focuses on peer helping and social status in a multi-age primary classroom.

Jill Wilmarth teaches 4th grade at Pine Ridge Elementary School in Stone Mountain, Georgia. She is working with her students on developing learning contracts and collaborative learning in social studies.

Index